February 2008

LAUNCHING A
LEADERSHIP
REVOLUTION

LAUNCHING A LEADERSHIP REVOLUTION

MASTERING THE FIVE LEVELS OF INFLUENCE

CHRIS BRADY | ORRIN WOODWARD

BUSINESS PLUS

NEW YORK BOSTON

Business Plus
Hachette Book Group USA
237 Park Avenue
New York, NY 10017

Visit our Web site at www.HachetteBookGroupUSA.com.

Business Plus is an imprint of Grand Central Publishing.
The Business Plus name and logo is a trademark of Hachette Book Group USA, Inc.

Printed in the United States of America
First Business Plus Edition: September 2007
10 9 8 7 6 5

Library of Congress Cataloging-in-Publication Data
Brady, Christopher
  Launching a leadership revolution : mastering the five levels of influence / Chris Brady and Orrin Woodward. — 1st ed.
      p. cm.
    Includes index.
    ISBN-13: 978-0-446-58071-7
    ISBN-10: 0-446-58071-6
  1. Leadership I. Woodward, Orrin. II. Title.
    HD57.7.B724 2007
    658.4'092—dc22   2007006043

Book design by Charles Sutherland

Revolutionary moments attract those who are not good enough for es-tablished institutions as well as those who are too good for them.

—George Bernard Shaw

The greatest revolution of our generation is the discovery that human beings, by changing the inner attitudes of their minds, can change the outer aspects of their lives. —William James

Twenty years from now you will be more disappointed by the things that you didn't do than by the ones you did do. So throw off the bowlines. Sail away from the safe harbor. Catch the trade winds in your sails. Ex-plore. Dream. Discover. —Mark Twain

Revolution is not a dinner party. —Sun Yat-sen

ACKNOWLEDGMENTS

When writing a book such as this, authors run the risk of appearing as if they think they know everything. Before the reader jumps to any such conclusion, allow us the disclaimer that we struggle daily to implement and improve our abilities with the concepts contained in these pages. The material presented here is not theory, but rather real-life experience from the perspective of two businessmen who must live it every day. We have experienced much and learned even more in over a decade of business enterprise together, and would have been helped significantly along the way had the information in these pages been available in this form. For that reason, we decided to write this book.

The second risk run by authors is appearing to work alone. Nothing could be further from the truth. We are indebted to many writers and leaders both contemporary and deceased, speakers, teachers, and mentors from whom we've drawn heavily. The bibliography at the back of this book lists those from whom we've selected quotes and major material concepts. In particular, we wish to salute John Maxwell and Jim Collins for illuminating the idea of Leadership Levels. We don't know which, if either, first penned the concept, but we have been inspired by the profound insight and perspective provided by both. High on the list of those to whom we owe gratitude is our patient editor and literary mentor Rick Wolff. He has shown us a whole new world of which we are glad to be a part. We also want to thank our friend Pastor Robert Dickie for his spiritual mentorship and friendship throughout the years; his example is the best sermon of all. Our wives, Terri Brady and Laurie Woodward, who somehow manage to be beautiful, loving, flexible, understanding, and encouraging all at the same time, deserve our special thanks and gratitude. Additional thanks goes to Terri Brady for painstaking supervision of the early editing of this manuscript. We are also indebted to our business partners Tim Marks and Larry Van BusKirk for keen insights that made the book much better. Thanks also are due Russ Mack for believing in the big picture of this manuscript from the beginning. Chris wants to thank his parents, Jim and Gayle Brady, and Orrin wishes to thank his parents, Bud (deceased) and Kathy Woodward, for their constant belief and encouragement. Norm Williams, our graphic designer and artist, deserves recognition for responding patiently to our many directives and ongoing changes. We would also like to give a nod to all the hours contributed by Bob Dickie III and his staff, and to Doug and Tiffany Huber, who have faithfully served in various capacities behind the scenes.

Most importantly, we wish to give all glory to our Lord and Savior, Jesus Christ. Everything we have and will ever accomplish is by His grace.

CONTENTS

INTRODUCTION

J ust before the Great Depression a man named Ira Yates sold his profitable business to return to the ranching life he had known growing up. He bought a thousand acres in west Texas and struggled through the years of the Depression, barely able to make a living. As he heard rumors of Texas oil fields being discovered, he decided to drill on his ranch, but had difficulty getting oil companies to assist him with the complicated process. Finally, Yates set up a test rig and found that he was living above one of the largest oil fields in North America. His fortune was made.

Leadership ability is a lot like the drilling equipment used by Yates and his partners to discover the richness of oil that already existed beneath him. Each of us has a natural wellspring of talent and ability buried within. The drill of leadership is required to tap into the geyser of our potential. As with Yates's drilling equipment, leadership ability will take effort to attain, but the rewards are incalculable.

Everyone is called upon to lead in some capacity sooner or later in life. Some of the issues involved are big, some are small. Sometimes the responsibilities requiring leadership last a lifetime, and sometimes they are needed only for a moment. Leadership, then, is something each of us should strive to understand better and utilize more fully. Whether in a corporate setting, a business of our own, a church environment, a volunteer organization, or in the home, improving our leadership abilities through the development process described in this book is key to unleashing the potential hidden within. Helping to guide others through the same process is the secret to collective greatness and organizational victories.

Increasing our ability to lead requires change. Vital to tapping into our inner wells of potential are the willingness and ability to grow personally and organizationally. James C. Hunter wrote, "I never cease to be amazed that organizations do not insist that their leaders be continually improving and persistently working toward becoming the best leaders they can be. With the awesome responsibility of leading others and the high stakes involved, it seems obvious to me that organizations would focus their attention on helping their leaders develop their leadership skills and thereby their character."

We wrote this book because our work with tens of thousands of entrepreneurs across North America for more than a decade has convinced us that most people (and their organizations) have much more potential locked away inside of them than they realize. Leadership is the key that opens the lock on that potential. Time and again we have seen people come alive and achieve things they never thought possible, once they started learning to take responsibility for leadership. The results, quite frankly, have been *revolutionary*.

Noel Tichy wrote, "In a broad sense, what leaders do is stage revolutions." The term *revolution* is defined by Webster as "an activity or movement designed to effect fundamental changes." In the beginning, revolutions begin with unrest on the part of one person or perhaps a small group of individuals. These early leaders begin working to influence events in a direction that assaults the status quo. Things can no longer remain as they were. Changes must be made. Usually because of their passion for the ideals espoused by the leaders, other people are drawn into the effort. Gradually, the strivings of these early "initiators" gain momentum, attracting talent and support from broader and broader areas. As a tiny campfire grows into a large bonfire with increased fuel and oxygen supply, so too does a revolution grow in power and potency as fundamental changes are made and the results of those changes begin to surface.

Sometimes a bonfire ends up engulfing the woods around it as it grows into a forest fire. It can never be forgotten, though, that all big fires start with a tiny spark. Similarly, all revolutions start as small rebellions. The root cause can always be traced back to a single individual or idea. Fundamental changes are wrought because somewhere, somehow, for some reason, someone provided leadership. One person can decide to lead. One person can make a difference. One person leading does make a difference.

True leadership can bring radically positive change to a stagnant environment. It can revitalize old relationships, poorly performing organizations, and underachieving individuals. Leadership blows in like a fresh wind and clears the cobwebs of complacency. For most organizations, management is common and leadership is rare. Our experience has been that, all too often, where good leadership is needed, poor management is there as an imposter. Leadership and management are two very different concepts. Leadership is about doing the right things; management is about doing those things in the right way. Both are vital, but each has its place. Any group, any organization, any cause can be revitalized with proper leadership, but never with great management. Leadership must come first. Therefore, whether initiating a new venture or turning around an existing one, *Launching a Leadership Revolution* is the first and most important step to success.

In this book, ideas and principles of leadership will be presented in ascending "levels" to illustrate the crescendo effect of increased leadership ability. It will become clear that as an individual or organization grows in leadership effectiveness, so too will the results, which will gain power and force like a fire burning brighter and brighter—or, more illustratively, like a *revolution*. Additionally, each chapter is punctuated with an example from history to show how its principles have been applied in real-life situations. As author Barry Lopez wrote, "Sometimes a person needs a story more than food to stay alive." The stories that history tells are often more interesting and enlightening than hours of expository teaching.

Life should be about purpose and meaning and cause and fulfilling our personal, God-given destinies. Without exception, this is achieved through, with, and for *people*. In other words, it's done through leadership. Writer Ken Kesey states, "You don't lead by pointing a finger and telling people some place to go. You lead by going to that place and making a case." It is our intention that this book will go to a certain place and make a compelling case. The *place* is the wellspring of your personal potential, and that of your organization. The *case* we wish to make is that your potential is bountiful and sufficient to fulfill your life's calling. It sits there now, waiting to be tapped. This is accomplished by taking responsibility to lead in the areas of your life where you have been called. As you grow in your leadership ability, you will revolutionize your life.

May the pages that follow serve to enlighten, instruct, edify, teach, and encourage, but most of all may they inspire you to set up a drill rig of leadership in your life and/or organization and harvest the abundance buried within.

We wish you all the success you are prepared to earn.

Happy drilling.

Let the revolution begin.

—Chris Brady and Orrin Woodward
Fall 2006

WHAT A LEADER IS

CHAPTER 1

Leadership Discussion

Sometimes if you want to see a change for the better, you have to take things into your own hands.

—CLINT EASTWOOD

A Question of Leadership

We find ourselves in a time when leadership is sorely needed. From the chaos, confusion, and rampant mediocrity that we find in our schools, churches, workplaces, families, personal lives, national politics, and international relations, the same questions seem to echo: "Will somebody please lead?" "Isn't there anybody who can fix this?" "Is there anyone who can make sense of all this?" "Is there anyone who cares enough to take responsibility for improvement here?" "Where are the leaders?" "Do heroes even exist anymore?"

These questions and more flow freely. Everybody seems to have an innate sense that something is needed. It is not hard to identify problems in a given situation. Ask someone to identify what's wrong with their church, employer, or neighbors and you'd better be prepared for a long explanation. Don't even get them started on the government! That could take days. Identifying negatives and areas for improvement is child's play. Making suggestions for changes and modifications is not difficult, either. Everyone has an opinion about how to make improvements. Coming up with good ideas is no big deal. The world is full of great ideas and deep thinkers of grand theories. Implementation and results make the difference. They separate the heroes from the rest. And implementation with results, in any field or endeavor, takes leadership.

What Is Leadership?

The concept of "leadership" is a complex one. Most everybody has a feel for what the term means, at least in a general sense, but generalizations about leadership don't help us very much. In order to understand how to lead and why to lead and what it even means to lead, we'd better get clear on what comprises this complex idea embodied in this simple little English word.

We've tried this exercise of defining leadership with audiences large and small, and invariably the same thing happens. We begin getting word phrases that all sound pretty good, phrases like "taking responsibility" and "getting results," or one-word descriptors such as "commitment," "perseverance," "charisma," and "integrity." These are all true in a sense, but somehow they don't go far enough. So then we switch to attempting definitions by combining all these phrases, but it creates so much mumbo jumbo, like one big buzzword soup from a corporate boardroom. Somehow the words meant something to us individually when thinking about leadership, but when fused together the life went right out of them.

At this point it may be helpful to turn to some experts on the subject. Surely they can bring some congruity. The list that follows is just a short offering:

1. James C. Hunter: "We define leadership . . . as a skill of influencing people to work enthusiastically toward goals identified as being for the common good."
2. Al Kaltman: "The successful leader gets superior performance from ordinary people."
3. Bill George: "The leader's job is to provide an empowering environment that enables employees to serve their customers and provides them the training, education, and support they need."
4. Andy Stanley: "Leaders provide a mental picture of a preferred future and then ask people to follow them there."
5. Vance Packard: "Leadership is getting others to want to do something that you are convinced should be done."
6. Garry Wills: "Leadership is mobilizing others toward a goal shared by the leader and followers."
7. Alan Keith: "Leadership is ultimately about creating a way for people to contribute to making something extraordinary happen."
8. George Barna: "A leader is one who mobilizes; one whose focus is influencing people; a person who is goal driven; someone who has an orientation in common with those who rely upon him for leadership; and someone who has people willing to follow them," and "Leadership is the process of motivating, mobilizing, resourcing, and directing people to passionately and strategically pursue a vision from God that a group jointly embraces."
9. Kenneth O. Gangel: "I consider leadership to be the exercise of one's special gifts under the call of God to serve

a certain group of people in achieving the goals God has given them toward the end of glorifying Christ."

10. Dwight D. Eisenhower: "Leadership is the art of getting someone else to do something you want done because he wants to do it."

These insights and definitions are good and helpful, and some we like particularly, but John Maxwell gives an exemplary definition, quoted here at length from his book *The 21 Irrefutable Laws of Leadership*:

> Leadership is influence—nothing more, nothing less. People have so many misconceptions about leadership. When they hear that someone has an impressive title or an assigned leadership position, they assume that he is a leader. Sometimes that's true. But titles don't have much value when it comes to leading. True leadership cannot be awarded, appointed, or assigned. It comes only from influence, and that can't be mandated. It must be earned.

What, then, is *influence*? Our favorite explanation of influence comes to us from nineteenth-century preacher and author Albert Barnes: "Influence is that in a man's known talents, learning, character, experience, and position, on which a presumption is based that what he holds is true; that what he proposes is wise."

George Barna tells us, "To be effective, a leader must have influence. But influence is a *product* of great leadership; it is *not* synonymous with it. You can have influence in a person's life without leading him anywhere."

Perhaps there will never be a short, cute definition for leadership. We are certain there will never be one upon which all "experts" agree. This very difficulty in arriving at a concise explanation for the concept illustrates the enormity of the subject at hand. But all of the above definitions hit near the same mark.

Any attempts to be more concise or specific are like trying to grab smoke. For the purpose of this study, then, we will fuse the above commentary into the following:

Leadership is the influence of others in a productive, vision-driven direction and is done through the example, conviction, and character of the leader.

Why Leadership?

We have surveyed the thoughts of many great minds on the definition of leadership and, as with a complex painting, the image is getting clearer the more we work with it. To brush in more detail, we must discuss the *purpose* of leadership.

Many people are interested in leadership for what they imagine it can provide them, including:

1. Power
2. Control
3. Perks or Being Served.

But the life of a leader is quite different from such expectations. The life of a leader involves:

1. Giving power (empowering)
2. Helping others fix problems and move forward
3. Serving others.

Leaders lead for the joy of creating something bigger than themselves. Noted leadership consultant Warren Bennis says that he wants to publish books "that disturb the present in the service of a better future." That's good, and it's a sentiment shared by Hyrum Smith: "Leaders conduct planned conflict against the status quo."

To illustrate, consider the story of Ray Kroc and the making of the McDonald's fast-food empire. Kroc discovered the little McDonald's restaurant in Southern California in the 1950s and was amazed. The McDonald brothers had developed an efficient, unique, and highly profitable operation. They had fast-food production and delivery down to a science, and they were making what they considered a lot of money. But Kroc saw further. He realized that their little restaurant could be copied and duplicated and reproduced around the nation, and he set about trying to make that happen. Author Jim Collins, in *Good to Great*, explained that great leaders have ambition beyond their own personal self-interest. They are not satisfied with personal success only, but focus almost entirely upon furthering the vision of the *enterprise*.

> *Leaders can't stand to leave things the way they found them.*

At first Kroc attempted partnering with the McDonald brothers, but he found this restrictive and an anchor on his progress. Then he tried buying rights to their system for a period of ten years, but again, his vision outran theirs and he found the provisions contained within the contract to be incompatible with his vision. Maury Klein explains what happened in *The Change Makers*: "As that vision expanded, [Kroc] found the brothers unwilling to deviate from the strict letter of the original terms." The best explanation, however, comes from Kroc himself: "The McDonald brothers were simply not on my wavelength at all. I was obsessed with the idea of making McDonald's the biggest and best. They were content with what they had." The McDonald brothers were content. Kroc was not.

So if leadership is influence applied toward an overarching vision (pun intended), it follows that this influence is motivated by discontent with the status quo and directed toward something better. We like to call this "making a difference." And leaders do that in the direction of their vision for the future, a vision that sees farther than others see. George Barna says, "[Leaders] have to own the vision completely. It must be a perception of a coming reality to which [they] are totally committed." Leaders can't stand to leave things the way they found them. They are driven to make them better. It is from this discontent, and toward their vision, with ownership and commitment, that they exercise influence. According to President Theodore Roosevelt, "We need leaders of inspired idealism, leaders to whom are granted great visions, who dream greatly and strive to make their dreams come true; who can kindle the people with the fire from their own burning souls." That is what it means to *lead*.

Results

The level of leadership determines the success of its results. Over time, where there are lackluster results, there is a leadership deficiency. Where there are stellar results, there is strong leadership. John Maxwell says that "everything rises and falls on leadership."

Let's first consider the results of *poor leadership*.

When leaders or those in a position to lead shirk their responsibilities, cut corners, or fail in their responsibilities, the results are far reaching. Says Bill George in *Authentic Leadership*, "A Time/CNN poll taken in the summer of 2002 reported that 71 percent of those polled feel that the 'typical CEO is less honest and ethical than the average person.' In rating the moral and ethical standards of CEOs of major corporations, 72 percent rated them 'fair' or 'poor.' A similar survey by the *Wall Street Journal Europe* reported that only 21 percent of European investors believe that corporate leaders are honest." So one of the first products of poor leadership is an erosion of the trust people have in those who should be leading. As author Les Csorba wrote in *Trust*, "Leadership is character in motion."

Next come pain and suffering, which can be on a corporate,

financial, or emotional level, depending on the setting. Or they may have major geopolitical ramifications.

The War of 1812 was a perilous time for the brand-new United States. Only a few decades old, the young country found itself embroiled in yet another war with England. With the exception of a very impressive string of naval victories, the United States had been battered at the hands of the British. Washington, the national capital that was still under construction, had been not only successfully invaded but also humiliatingly burned. While a treaty of sorts had been signed between the two nations, the British knew that word of the peace would not travel fast enough to stop the invading force they'd sent to attack the city of New Orleans.

New Orleans was a strategically pivotal city. Most of the trade from the North American west flowed down the Mississippi and through New Orleans at the base of the river's delta. If New Orleans were lost, Britain believed it could split the United States in half and force a treaty more favorable to their side. With the positive conclusion of an invasion of New Orleans, there would be time for the British parliament to reject the current terms and negotiate a much stiffer peace.

The confidence of the New Orleans leadership to fend off an attack was receding like an ebb tide. The Committee for the Safety of New Orleans issued a report itemizing the poor morale and lack of preparations by the local militia in defense of the city. The city had transferred from the hands of the Spanish, then the French, and finally to the United States in less than a decade, and the loyalty of her defenders was a major concern. In fact, the speaker of the Louisiana senate considered surrendering the city to the British without a fight because most inhabitants were more loyal to the city than to the United States. Additionally, there was the very real fear of a slave rebellion in the area.

By contrast, the British were confident. Riding high on their victory in the Napoleonic Wars, they expected a decisive rout at

New Orleans. Many veterans of Wellington's victorious army of Waterloo were in the invading army's ranks. They were battle tested and proven, and certainly no ragtag multicultural militia could match their might.

If the leadership of New Orleans' defenses had remained in this confused state, the British hopes would have been well founded. The tumult in New Orleans would have given way to the armies of the British just as it had in Washington. One can only guess what would have become of the infantile United States had it been split in half from its south.

In the case of the defense of New Orleans in the War of 1812, the tragedy of poor leadership is quite clear. The results are similar to the results of bad leadership elsewhere, though they may not be fatal, whether in industry, in politics, or in the home. Chaos, lack of progress, confusion, and frustration are sure to follow where leaders refuse or fail to lead.

Now let's observe *real leadership* in action by resuming our look at the Battle of New Orleans.

Into this storm marched Major General Andrew Jackson. Only Andrew Jackson's indomitable will and courageous leadership stood between an acceptable peace treaty and the potential destruction of the United States. With only his small Tennessee militia, Jackson arrived on the scene just in time to bring order out of chaos and resolve out of fear. Assuming leadership of a patchwork army made up of the Louisiana militia, a band of local pirates, and several hundred black volunteers from Haiti, Jackson's entire force amounted to just over half the total available to the British invaders.

General Jackson immediately took charge. He declared martial law in the city and imposed a strict curfew. When he was alerted to the British landing less than a day's march from New Orleans, he mobilized his forces into action. Instead of waiting for the British to march to the city, Jackson devised a surprise attack. Had

Jackson waited and allowed the British soldiers to assault the city on their own terms, the fragile confidence the New Orleans populace had in Jackson's ability to stop the British would have been destroyed. Instead, the surprise attack from the Americans pinned down the British and stopped their advance in its tracks. The battle would take place right where Jackson decided it would.

Quick and creative defense works allowed Jackson's badly outnumbered and outclassed army to perform at a level way above its strength. The battle opened with an intense artillery barrage, but Jackson's personal courage steeled the resolve of his men to endure in the face of overwhelming odds. Intense combat followed as the heroes of Europe slammed their best troops against Jackson's forces. Jackson shrewdly deployed his troops to meet every British challenge, much of the early fighting turning into hand-to-hand slugfests. Unable to advance and suffering heavy losses, the British lines eventually gave way. The battle turned into a rout. Three top British generals were killed in what became the most lopsided battle of the war. Within a few hundred yards lay nearly one thousand dead and dying British. The American side suffered thirteen killed and wounded.

The Battle of New Orleans, as it came to be called, allowed the treaty ending the conflict to be ratified and the War of 1812 to end. The difference between the early pessimism of the New Orleans defenders and the final American result was due directly to the leadership and decision making of General Andrew Jackson.

It was the same company, the same men, the same battle, the same enemy, but a different leader that dramatically turned the tide. The strength of the leadership makes all the difference.

Cultivating Leadership

So how does one acquire leadership? The very asking of that question presupposes a very important first point: Leadership ability can be acquired. Some say leaders are born, that they come into the world with natural abilities. This is certainly true to some degree. Others say leadership can be learned.

The truth is that anybody can develop his leadership ability beyond his current level. A good analogy for this is muscular strength and development. Certainly some people are born with more robust physiques than others, but every person has the potential and ability to work on that God-given physique to strengthen and tone the muscles. No matter how big or small, how strong or weak, every individual can work to improve his or her condition.

> *Anybody can grow in leadership ability.*

Leadership can be considered in the same way. While people may exhibit differing natural levels of leadership, *everybody* can cultivate and grow his or her leadership ability. Besides, ability differs from one endeavor to the next, so that a person may have weak influence in one area but be strong in another. Everybody can be a leader at something, and usually people's strengths lie in areas that interest them greatly. So the very fact that you are interested in developing stronger leadership abilities in a particular area probably means you have some degree of natural ability there already. This may not always be the case, but we observe it to be true quite often. In *The Leadership Challenge*, authors Kouzes and Posner wrote, "What we have discovered, and rediscovered, is that leadership is not the private reserve of a few charismatic men and women. It is a process ordinary people use when they are bringing forth the best from themselves and others. What we've discovered is that people make extraordinary things happen by liberating the leader within everyone."

So the strategy is to cultivate and develop leadership ability within ourselves. We need to understand that leadership can and must be developed, even for the most "gifted." This is done on purpose. Change is always present, but growth and improvement are optional. Leadership development is a deliberate process.

The leadership-development process begins by finding a source of leadership and wisdom in a particular area of interest. Training and growth begin by associating with those who have reached the "fruit on the tree." Would-be leaders should look to where the fruit hangs on the tree and then learn from those who have obtained results. Author Stevenson Willis wrote, "Seek . . . the counsel of those who have achieved the goal for which you strive; for in all matters, the words of one who has prospered are far weightier than the words of one who has not."

We will discuss this in more detail later in the book. At this point suffice it to say that leadership can and must be developed, and it occurs deliberately at the direction of someone who is already accomplished in that area. That is both the right way and the shortest way to develop leadership ability.

Art and Science

The essence of leadership cannot easily be classified or codified or served up in some ready-to-order fashion. We believe the reason for this difficulty lies in the very makeup of leadership itself. You see, there are those who claim that leadership is an "art." In *Leaders on Leadership* Doug Murren says, "A leader is more of an artist than a scientist or a politician; leadership itself is an art form." Being an art, it would come easily to people with the right "talent." Others claim that there is no art to being a great leader and that it is entirely learnable. Still others split these claims down the middle, observing that good leadership is part art and part science. We agree with this middle road. It is difficult to define exactly what a leader is, but we recognize a good one when he or she shows up!

So leadership is part *art* and part *science*. This means that leadership involves "presuppositions," which are the thought processes, mind-sets, or mentalities upon which a leader operates.

This is the "art" side of leadership. Resting atop those mentalities is the "science" side, or what leaders actually "do." These are the actions and strategies of leadership. Together, blending art and science, we begin to get a picture of what leadership really is. According to author James Strock, "Leadership, built on the hard ground of truth, also requires artistry to reach the summit."

Just as both artists and scientists can develop their abilities, so too can leaders develop theirs: hence the purpose of this book. The following chapters seek to aid the reader in developing as a leader. We will begin with some prerequisites that all leaders must have before advancing, then discuss the overall Cycle of Achievement that serves as a feedback loop the leader will experience while in pursuit of growth. The book will crescendo to a finale with the Five Levels of Leadership.

What a Leader Is: Winston Churchill and "Britain's Finest Hour"

It began with what were called the "bloodless" conquests: the Rhineland, Austria, the Sudetenland, Czechoslovakia, and then Memel in Lithuania. These countries and territories fell to Nazi Germany without so much as a whimper. The British prime minister and the French premier, at a meeting with Adolf Hitler in Munich in September of 1938, were said to "fairly fall over themselves to agree with Hitler" to carve up the former Czechoslovakian Republic. As a result of this shameless pacification, "a prosperous industrial nation was split up and bankrupted overnight," in the words of William Shirer in *The Rise and Fall of the Third Reich*, and Czechoslovakia's free people were placed under the dominion of one of history's most ruthless megalomaniacs. As Hitler himself commented, "Czechoslovakia had ceased to exist." Returning home to England from Munich, British prime minister Neville Chamberlain bragged erroneously that "it is peace in our time."

For nearly six years there had been one voice in the darkness crying out against this blind appeasement. The voice spoke out vehemently and often. The voice spoke loudly. The voice warned continually of the threat of the growing Nazi power and predicted the shrewd moves of Hitler's conquests again and again. The man behind the voice: Winston Churchill.

A former member of Parliament, a former first lord of the Admiralty, and an extremely active member of British government during World War I, Churchill had been out of the government since 1929. In terms of position or authority, he was powerless. He had none of the influence of public office. He had no official leverage upon the policies of his government. Nevertheless, as Martin Gilbert made clear in *Churchill: A Life*, he did everything he could to inform, persuade, and convince his countrymen of the dangers facing not only England, but all of Europe. "Asking me not to make a speech [about the dangers in Europe]," Churchill said, "is like asking a centipede to get along and not put a foot on the ground." Of the cowardly actions of the neutral states in the face of Nazi aggression Churchill said, "Each one hopes that if it feeds the crocodile enough, the crocodile will eat him last."

According to William Shirer, "Winston Churchill, in England, alone seemed to understand. No one stated the consequences of Munich more succinctly than he in his speech to the Commons of October 5: 'We have sustained a total and unmitigated defeat . . . And do not suppose that this is the end. It is only the beginning.' "

Hitler's next step was to form an alliance with Mussolini, the bloodthirsty dictator of Italy, in what would be called the Pact of Steel. Following that, he signed an agreement of mutual non-aggression with Russia. Adolf Hitler had systematically built up his strength and eliminated the threats of those strong enough to stop him. As a result, his language grew bolder. In a talk to his military chiefs, Hitler said:

> I shall give a propagandist reason for starting the war—never mind whether it is plausible or not. The victor will not be asked afterward whether he told the truth or not. In starting and waging a war it is not right that matters, but victory. Close your hearts to pity! Act brutally! The stronger man is right. . . . Be harsh and remorseless! Be steeled against all signs of compassion! . . . Whoever has pondered over this world order knows that its meaning lies in the success of the best by means of force.

The individual countries of Europe were at the disposal of a deranged man who would utter such words as these, and only slowly was the world waking up to the danger.

Then on September 1, 1939, over a million and a half German troops crossed the border into peaceful Poland and invaded. The world was now awake. Within days, England and France finally declared war on Germany. Almost immediately, Winston Churchill was called back into government service as the first lord of the Admiralty.

Eight short months later, on the morning of May 10, 1940, Germany simultaneously invaded Holland, Belgium, and France. Churchill was named prime minister by nightfall that same day. He later would write how when he went to bed that night he was conscious "of a profound sense of relief. At last I had authority to give directions over the whole scene. I felt as if I were walking with destiny, and that all my past life had been but a preparation for this hour and for this trial."

The man Europe had ignored had been put in the driver's seat at the last desperate minute. Western civilization had been crumbling under a severe lack of leadership. Now that lack of leadership was ending.

Winston Churchill took the reins of authority with vigor. On the afternoon of May 13, just three days after becoming prime minister, Churchill summoned his ministers and told them, "I have nothing to offer but blood, toil, tears and sweat." Then in front of the entire Commons he said:

> You ask what is our policy? I will say: It is to wage war, by sea, land and air, with all our might and with all the strength that God can give us; to wage war against a monstrous tyranny, never surpassed in the dark, lamentable catalogue of human crime. That is our policy.
>
> You ask what is our aim? I can answer in one word: victory, victory at all costs, victory in spite of all terror, victory, however long and hard the road may be; for without victory there is no survival. Let that be realized; no survival for the British Empire, no survival for all that the British Empire has stood for, no survival for the urge and impulse of the ages, that mankind will move forward towards its goals.
>
> But I take up my task with buoyancy and hope. I feel sure that our cause will not be suffered to fail among men. At this time I feel entitled to claim the aid of all, and I say, "Come then, let us go forward together with our united strength."

Then France, Belgium, and Holland all fell to Nazi forces. At the shores of Dunkirk in early June, nearly 350,000 British and French soldiers had to be rescued by a daring and heroic sea evacuation moments before they would have been crushed by the advancing German army. In a speech addressed primarily to Germany and Italy (confided Churchill to U.S. president Roosevelt), Churchill was at his inspirational best:

> Even though large tracts of Europe and many old and famous States have fallen or may fall into the grip of the Gestapo and all the odious apparatus of Nazi rule, we shall not flag or fail.
>
> We shall go on to the end. We shall fight in France, we shall fight on the seas and oceans, we shall fight with growing confi-

dence and growing strength in the air, we shall defend our island, whatever the cost may be.

We shall fight on the beaches, we shall fight on the landing grounds, we shall fight in the fields and in the streets, we shall fight in the hills; we shall never surrender.

According to Martin Gilbert, "Churchill paid no attention to . . . doom. His mind was made up; the defeatism of others could not change his intention." As it was obvious that France had been totally defeated, Churchill said:

I expect that the Battle of Britain is about to begin. Upon this battle depends the survival of Christian civilization. Upon it depends our own British life and the long continuity of our institutions and our Empire. The whole fury and might of the enemy must very soon be turned on us. Hitler knows that he will have to break us in this island or lose the war. If we can stand up to him, all Europe may be free, and the life of the world may move forward into broad, sunlit uplands; but if we fail, then the whole world, including the United States, and all that we have known and cared for, will sink into the abyss of a new dark age made more sinister, and perhaps more protracted, by the lights of a perverted science. Let us therefore brace ourselves to our duty and so bear ourselves that if the British Empire and its Commonwealth last for a thousand years, men will say, "This was their finest hour."

The Battle of Britain had indeed begun. German planes began bombing eastern England, targeting highly populated civilian areas to strike fear and terror into the masses. Innocent people died by the tens of thousands. The United States would not enter the war for almost another year and a half. Britain was alone.

Winston Churchill, however, was a real leader. He had an all-consuming cause that guided his steps, and the confidence of a man who knows he was destined for that moment in time. His fortitude, his confidence, his determination, his constant ebullient communications to his countrymen somehow held things together. The tiny little island fought like a caged lion and somehow hung on. Eventually the United States was drawn into the war by Japan, and the fascist countries one by one were defeated by the allies.

As Martin Gilbert wrote, "[Churchill's] personal inspiration was itself an element in Britain's war-making powers." *That's* leadership.

Leadership can also be recognized by the results it generates. Churchill assembled a very effective War Cabinet and efficiently increased the ability of his nation to produce war munitions and equipment. He forged secret supply agreements with the United States. Gilbert wrote, "A remarkable war-making instrument was in place; Churchill, with his forceful energy, his long experience and his unswerving faith in a victorious outcome, provided it with the impetus and the fire." The result was that Churchill's England held tough against a massive and unrelenting German onslaught. *That's* leadership.

An enduring legacy is also pure evidence of leadership. Most historians agree: The years of World War II, and especially the early ones including the Battle of Britain, are indeed "Britain's finest hour." For a country with such a rich and long history, that is really saying something. Again, *that's* leadership.

Leadership is a deep and fascinating subject. Leaders come in all shapes and sizes and from all walks of life. Throughout this book we will explain it and teach it, but if ever anyone desired a simple portrait of leadership instead of all the words, one should simply picture portly, sixty-something Winston Churchill standing defiantly amidst the rubble of a bombed-out and nearly ruined London, cigar clenched firmly between his teeth and stubby fingers thrust confidently in the air signifying "victory." Providing a mental picture of a preferred future, mobilizing others toward a common goal, influencing them in a productive, vision-driven direction, Churchill was the perfect example of the conviction and character of a leader.

WHAT A LEADER BRINGS

CHAPTER 2

Foundational Qualities

Study while others are sleeping; work while others are loafing; prepare while others are playing; and dream while others are wishing.

—WILLIAM A. WARD

The journey into the center of this concept called leadership has only just begun. Everything we've discussed so far can be thought of as a road map, one that provided guidance to the location where an understanding of leadership can be discovered. Arriving in that place, we must next open a door to a structure that presents leadership as a series of ascending stairs. Gaining access to the base of those stairs is what this chapter is all about. Before anyone can begin ascending the stairs of leadership success, he or she must possess the correct combination to open the door.

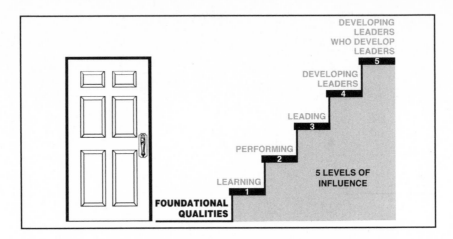

This combination to entry is comprised of the Three Hs. These three characteristics of "raw material" for a leader are:

1. Hungry
2. Hone-able
3. Honorable

These are the foundational qualities of a leader, the Three Hs that must be possessed by the leader-to-be as a prerequisite to further advancement. It is futile to proceed in leadership development without these cornerstones. One cannot begin climbing the stairs until one enters the room where the staircase begins.

Foundational Quality 1: Hungry

A leader is driven to change the status quo. As we discussed in the previous chapter, a leader is not just unhappy with things as they are, he or she must also want to change them for the better. This discontent produces the ambition or motivation to press forward and strive toward change. Some call it the will to win. Author John MacArthur writes: "All gifted leaders seem to have an innate drive to win. Those who lack the winning instinct don't make very effective leaders."

Hunger itself is one of the biggest facets of leadership. Hunger provides the energy to begin, the stamina to persist, and the will to finish an en-

> *Hunger itself is one of the biggest facets of leadership.*

deavor. It is this hunger or ambition that births leadership. Leadership is not determined by one's birth, as they believed in Europe in the Middle Ages, nor is it determined by one's position, as many believe today; but rather it is determined by influence and performance. Hunger is its cause.

There is an equation that is analogous to this very idea of hunger:

Work = Force X Distance

This formula represents physical entities in nature and accurately describes how they operate. The Work done is a result of the Force multiplied by the Distance over which that Force functions. In the case of leadership, the Work done can be looked upon as the Results. The Force would be the Effort expended by the leader and his followers, and the Distance could be considered the Scope or Reach of the leadership over time or over people. Applying leadership terminology, then, to a law of physics, we would get:

Results or Influence = Effort X Scope or Reach

We can see that Effort plays a vital role, and Effort is the direct result of the hunger involved, and the greater the Effort, the greater the Results or Influence. If an individual is only marginally committed to achieving a certain goal, it is more than likely that the goal will never be accomplished. The Effort must be significant, and significant efforts come only from those who are significantly "hungry."

The legend is told of a young squire in the service of a great knight. The squire's lifelong ambition is someday to become a knight himself. Through the years, the knight trains the squire in techniques of battle and weaponry. Being young, the squire is impatient and is prone to ask the knight if he, the squire, is ready to officially become a knight yet. Tiring of these repeated questions, the great knight sends his squire high into the hills to seek out an old sage who had once been the greatest knight of all. After a long and arduous journey, the young squire finds the sage.

"I have been sent by my liege to seek your counsel. He has told me you can determine when I shall be worthy to become a knight."

The sage answers with silence but motions for the boy to follow him to the shore of a large mountain lake. Quietly they set out in a small boat until they reach the very center of the water.

"Submerge yourself in the water," commands the mysterious sage to the squire.

"Jump in?" asks the squire.

The sage simply nods. The squire leaps from the boat into the frigid mountain spring water. But before the boy can reemerge, the sage reaches into the water and grabs the squire's head, holding him under. The squire kicks furiously and grabs at the still strong arm of the sage, but to no avail. The seconds drag into minutes, and finally the fight is all but gone out of the squire. At that instant, the sage lifts the boy back into the boat.

Furious, gasping, fearful, and exhausted, the squire looks up at the sage.

"Why were you trying to kill me?"

"I wasn't. If I'd have tried to kill you, I'd have succeeded."

"What were you doing, then?" asked the squire incredulously.

"Teaching you."

"Some lesson! What exactly was I supposed to learn—that you're a crazy old coot?"

"Aye, that and more." The sage nodded serenely. "Let me ask you a question. When I had you submerged, what was going through your mind?"

The squire thought a moment, his anger subsiding a bit.

"Air, I thought. Air. I've got to get air or I'll die. That's all I was thinking."

"There you have it, then, young squire. When you want to be a knight as badly as you wanted that air, you'll become one."

This little story is an accurate depiction of what we might call "significant hunger." Certainly the squire was motivated by the threat on his own life. Although the story provides an illustration through an exaggeration, the moral is nonetheless clear. For anything lofty to be accomplished, one must be significantly motivated. A graphic way to represent ambition or hunger is as follows:

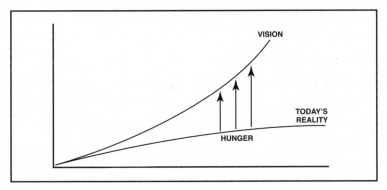

On this chart, today's reality is the bottom curve and the leader's vision of a better reality is the top curve. The gap between the two is hunger. This graph clearly shows that hunger grows as a seed in the soil of discontent, and stretches upward toward a better vision of tomorrow like a plant toward the sun.

Hunger as a Discipline

Those who take active responsibility to foster their motivation on a regular basis will outperform those who do not. It is the responsibility of the leader to keep him- or herself hungry on a regular basis. Napoleon Hill, author of the world-famous book *Think and Grow Rich*, said, "One must realize that all who have accumulated great fortunes first did a certain amount of dreaming, hoping, wishing, desiring, and planning *before* they acquired money."

All of leadership starts with hunger. At any point in time when the leader is not hungry, the leader is not functioning as a leader. This may sound radical, but it is true. Remember, a leader takes people somewhere. The moment the leader is not moving, the leader is not leading. And it takes ambition to keep the leader moving.

Picture success as a road that leads to your dreams:

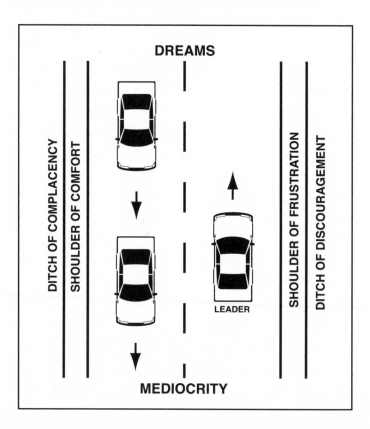

Along each side of the road are shoulders. Often the shoulders of roads are comprised of gravel. If a driver inadvertently runs onto the gravel, the sound serves as a warning that a course correction is required to resume traveling safely on the road. Conversely, sometimes that same gravel can grip the wheels of the vehicle and pull it from the road into the ditch.

On the left shoulder is *comfort*. Comfort is fine in small doses and in certain areas of life, but, like gravel, it can also serve as a warning. Remember, ambition flourishes in discontent with the status quo. Discontent and comfort cannot coexist. If a leader becomes too comfortable, ambition will die, and the soft gravel of comfort can pull him or her down into the Ditch of Complacency. *Complacency* is defined by Webster as "self-satisfaction accompanied by unawareness of actual dangers or deficiencies." Complacency pulls a leader from the road of success and halts all travel toward his or her dreams, as when a car is stuck in a ditch.

There is another danger in traveling too close to the shoulder of comfort: opposing traffic. Most people in life are looking for the easy road. They want comfort and will pay the price of mediocrity to get it, so they rush toward it like cows to the barn at feeding time. If a leader attempts to lead from a position of comfort, he or she will run smack into that mass of traffic heading in the other direction away from dreams and toward mediocrity.

Leaders, however, shun comfort and seek excellence instead. They subscribe to the theory held by author Al Kaltman: "Without meaningful work, life stinks." They travel down the right lane in the diagram and away from oncoming traffic. The right lane is never crowded. There always seems to be a shortage of leaders, but a plethora of people heading the other way. This is one thing that makes a leader so special. Also notice that being a leader means traveling close to the Shoulder of Frustration. In fact, this is the mark of any true leader. Being a leader is a study in managed frustration. How can one have ambition for a brighter tomorrow without being frustrated at the current set of realities? How can a leader be at war with the status quo and not be frustrated at the same time? The answer, of course, is that no leader can. Any real leader traveling the Road of Success toward his or her dreams will encounter frustration along the journey. Frustration can be healthy, but, just like the shoulder on the other side of the road, this gravel of frustration presents a trap. Too much frustration can be a warning to the leader that his or her attitude is dipping and could pull the leader down into the Ditch of Discouragement. Discouragement is a show-stopper because it robs the leader of hope. Without hope the leader is trapped in the Ditch of Discouragement and makes no further progress toward his or her dreams.

The only way to stay away from oncoming traffic, the Shoulder of Comfort, and the Ditch of Complacency—and the only way to travel near the Shoulder of Frustration but clear of the Ditch of Discouragement—is to focus straight ahead on the dreams in front of you. Having a dream-focus keeps a leader safely on the Road to Success. The best way to stay focused is to manage that hunger.

So staying hungry is actually a discipline. Webster defines discipline as "training that corrects, molds, or perfects the mental faculties." Hunger is certainly a mental faculty; notice that it needs training, molding, and perfecting. True leaders understand this and take the necessary steps on a regular basis to provide their hunger with the proper care and feeding. Many times leaders don't need to know more about *what* is to be done; they need to find more leverage for themselves to do what they already know how to do. How, exactly, is this done?

The Three Levels of Motivation

There are Three Levels of Motivation where hunger is fed and nurtured. The first is not quite as powerful as the second, and the second is not quite as powerful as the third.

Motivation Level 1: Material Success

This first category is comprised of all the material things that excite our senses and stimulate us to want to perform. For many people, one of the attractive aspects of performing as a leader in their field is the material or financial gain that can accompany that success. One doesn't have to look far or long for "things" that are desirable. Our modern commercial society is full of entertainments, trappings, rewards, and enticements that require money. Some people like nice cars and dream of buying that new convertible with the leather interior and sporty wheels. Others dream of building their own custom home suited to their exact specifications, perhaps on a nice remote parcel of land. Still others desire travel to exotic locations where they can meet interesting new people and sample regional cuisine. Attending professional sporting events in boxed seats, having enough money to alleviate debts, developing financial security, or retiring early are all common dreams. These and an endless list of other material rewards can and should be stimulating. The excitement about earning enough money to make these dreams a reality can serve as a level of motivation and fuel ambition. Author and speaker Anthony Robbins tells us, "If you get a big enough why, you can always figure out the how."

CONTRIBUTION AND CHARITABLE GIVING

A discussion on motivation at this level would be incomplete without pointing out that "material reward" can also provide for increased charitable giving. This is an exciting category for everyone who has causes that touch his or her heart. There are people in need every day. Perhaps one is concerned about the plight of the homeless in our land, or starving children in foreign countries, or those in crisis pregnancies, or battered wives, or orphaned children, or the severely disabled. Maybe there is a concern about the three little children down the road whose parents don't have enough money for Christmas. Perhaps one would like to donate money to a church for its outreach or missions programs. These causes all require two things: people who care and money.

With material success in the hands of those who care, significant differences can be made. Anybody's diet of dream-building should include time spent in the category of charitable giving. The Bible says, "It is more blessed to give than to receive" (Acts 20:35). Material success in the hands of good people who care increases the opportunity to experience this incredible law of life. Familiarizing oneself with the needs of others is a very important form of dream-building.

NEGATIVE MOTIVATIONS

Level 1 motivation is not always driven by positive rewards. It can also spring from negative realities. Anthony Robbins talks about the equally motivational forces of pain and pleasure.

Going back to our magnet example, we see that the negative can often times be as productive a force as the positive, propelling us away from some reality we wish to change. Still speaking of material issues, we can see how a lack of money could be a motivator. Others are motivated to achieve more success because they have a significant lack of time to spend with friends, family, and in community service. Some are so oppressed by debt and "negative" cash flow that they are sufficiently motivated. They are sick of borrowing from Peter to pay Paul, even at times getting all the apostles involved! The warning here, however, is not to dwell on these negative motivators too much. We would never want to induce depression! Clinical studies have proven that depression is not motivating.

Motivation Level 2: Recognition and Respect

The next level of motivation is comprised of recognition and respect. This is a deeper, more powerful level than that of material success.

RECOGNITION

It is a fact that in many cases people don't feel appreciated. Most crave the recognition that others can provide; a part of human nature is a deep need to be noticed and appreciated by others. In nearly any book in the category of "people skills," there will be paragraphs or entire chapters addressing the reasons to appreciate others and make them feel important. William James wrote, "The deepest principle in human nature is the craving to be appreciated." Charles Schwab, millionaire personnel expert during the Carnegie steel era (not to be confused with today's finance genius), said, "I have yet to find the person, however great or exalted his station, who did not do better work and put forth greater effort under a spirit of approval than he would ever do under a spirit of criticism."

It is no secret that everyone needs encouragement. For that reason, recognition by others is another healthy source of motivation. Perhaps one wishes to accomplish a level of achievement in business or at work because it drives public recognition. Maybe one wants the title that accompanies more responsibility at work or desires to win the plaque or trophy that is coveted in that field. These and other forms of recognition can and should be used as motivations for performance, as long as one's need for affirmation

> *"The deepest principle in human nature is the craving to be appreciated."*

from others does not grow too strong. Alas, as with all things, there are limits.

RESPECT

There is, however, a deeper level to this category of motivation. That deeper level is called respect. Much stronger than the need for simple recognition is the desire for somebody one respects to give respect in return.

Perhaps one wishes for a peer group at work or in business to observe and respect his or her accomplishments. Many people are motivated to obtain the respect of a mentor, parent, teacher, or boss. Still others seek the respect of their spouses. And at perhaps the deepest level in this category, there are those who are fighting for self-respect. Sometimes life can treat people harshly. They strive and fail repeatedly. They save for a rainy day and it floods. They climb the ladder of success only to find it leaning against the wrong wall. And over time, people build up a tremendous desire to win, to accomplish something that will prove to even themselves that they are valuable, that they can make it. Jane Haddam said, "In my day, we didn't have self-esteem, we had self-respect, and no more of it than we had earned." And, according to Axle Munthe, "A man can stand a lot as long as he can stand himself." These axioms ring true for many.

Another category of respect could be called "silencing the critics." The motivational aspects of this one are easy to see. How many ambitious performers have been stifled with criticism? How many of the great figures of history have had bellicose critics who cursed them at every turn? The answer? Almost all!

George Washington was criticized internationally as a young man when a copy of his personal, very private diary was found during an early skirmish with the French. It was printed in newspapers throughout Europe and meant to humiliate him. Henry Ford was called "greasy fingers." Benjamin Franklin was first criticized by colonists for being too European, then by Europeans for becoming a champion in the cause of liberty for the colonies. Ronald Reagan was called old, senile, economically reckless, was accused of sleeping through cabinet meetings and not grasping the complexities of geopolitical crises. Of Fred Astaire it was said, "Can't act. Can't sing. Slightly bald. Can dance a little." A Hollywood agent said of Lucille Ball, "Don't pay any attention to her. She's great at parties, but I can't see any future for her in movies." Napoleon said the Duke of Wellington, who would defeat him at Waterloo, was "a bad general and the English are bad soldiers." Gary Cooper said Clark Gable would "fall on his face" in his *Gone with the Wind* movie role. The manager of the Grand Ole Opry told Elvis Presley, "You ain't going nowhere, you ought to go back to driving a truck!" The Munich Technical Institute said of a young applicant named Albert Einstein, "Shows no promise." A millionaire businessman said of Charles Lindbergh and his flight across the Atlantic, "[He] will never make it. He's doomed." When Abraham Lincoln ran for reelection in 1864—just before he soundly defeated his challenger—a newspaper editor said, "Mr. Lincoln is already beaten. He cannot be re-elected." Of President Theodore Roosevelt it was said, "Roosevelt was the first president whose chief personal characteristic was mendacity, the first to glory in duplicity, the first braggart, the first bully, the first betrayer of a condemned for 'perpetual lying,' his shameless treatment of helpless women . . . and the civil strife that would almost inevitably ensue from patriotic resistance to usurpation by a half mad genius at the head of the proletariat."

Criticism is a fact of life for any performer, and it can be a great motivator to have someone telling you that you can't or shouldn't accomplish something. But, once again, don't take this too far. Chances are that no matter what you accomplish, you will not receive respect from critics. Why? Because giving respect is not their job. They are critics. If they ever stop criticizing, then by definition they cease being critics; they cease to exist. And nobody wants to cease to exist. So go ahead and perform. Prove the critics wrong. Use their doubts and negativism as a great motivator. *But look only to those you respect for respect.* Ignore the critics. Or, better yet, look at criticism as a sign that you are on the right track!

This yearning for respect that we've been discussing can be a strong motivator. It can exert more pull on us to perform than Level 1: Material Success. In fact, it is said that people will do more for respect and admiration than they will ever do for money. So find those

> **Look only to those you respect for respect.**

whom you admire, who are in a position in life you desire to be in, who are living their lives in a manner you wish to emulate, and strive to obtain their respect for what you are doing and accomplishing. That is one of the best routes to success. For when you obtain the respect of those who are where you want to be, you'll be on the path to where they are and what they have achieved.

A small warning: One should never become overly concerned with seeking the approval of other people. Ultimately, their approval or denial is something over which we have no control. It is simply recommended that leaders seek the approval of successful people who have set a good example, and who care about them and their success. This can be accomplished in a productive way when things are kept in balance.

Finally, and second only to pleasing God, self-respect should be pursued. Have your efforts resulted in the peace of mind that can only come from the knowledge that you did your personal best?

Motivation Level 3: Purpose, Destiny, and Legacy

PURPOSE

Material reward and contribution are exciting. Recognition and respect can be even bigger drivers, but by far the most sustaining, important, deep and durable motivation comes from a sense of purpose. Purpose is the "true north" for our mental and emotional inner compass. Purpose takes us out of the realm of living only for ourselves and our own selfish desires, and onto a higher plane. Purpose involves sacrifice for a greater good, contribution for making a bigger difference, and energies directed at a long-term view.

It has been said that "our purpose in life is to find a purpose in life." We are here for a reason. Our birth and development were not by mistake, nor the result of a series of cosmic accidents of chance. According to world-renowned macrobiologist and author Edgar Andrews in *From Nothing to Nature*, "Chance is the very opposite of purpose." Deep inside each one of us is the inner drive to accomplish something; in essence, to fulfill a purpose. J. Douglas Holladay said, "All of us seek to live lives that count. The big question that gnaws at us is: 'How can our lives truly make a difference?'"

Viktor Frankl said, "We do not determine our purpose, we detect it." One man likened this process of discovery to unearthing an important archeological artifact. The scientist carefully removes small layers of soil from the find. As the time-consuming process pro-

> **"We do not determine our purpose, we detect it."**

gresses, more and more of the artifact becomes visible and more and more can be learned about it, until the entire object is fully unearthed and displayed to the world. Individually, our purposes in life are a lot like that. We may feel for years as though we are digging for it. This can often be a slow and painstaking process. But, sticking to the search, eventually we start to uncover small bits and pieces of what God has built and equipped us to do. As we explore further our purpose becomes clearer. And, hopefully, if we work diligently toward answers, the full purpose is disclosed and enthusiastically embraced. This is vitally important. As General Douglas MacArthur said, "Every man should be embarrassed to die until he accomplishes something great in this world."

DESTINY

Destiny takes purpose further, comprehending the spiritual component. Destiny says that we were created, created for a purpose, and the unique abilities and opportunities that we find in our lives are God-given. Who you are, where you live, the talents you were born with, the opportunities that have and will come your way, are all part of a bigger picture, a picture into which you were painted to fulfill a part that only you can fulfill.

You may find this hard to accept, thinking that perhaps life is a bundle of chance occurrences. We understand such skepticism and respect the right people have to it. But as our good friend Tim Marks says, "Be sure you know why you believe what you believe." Our study of history has shown again and again that, as Benjamin Franklin said at the Constitutional Convention that shaped our nation, "God governs in the affairs of men." George W. Bush said he felt as though he was being called to the presidency, that he had a "charge to keep." In his book, *A Charge to Keep*, Bush said he was inspired by the words in a hymn written by Charles Wesley:

> A charge to keep I have,
> A God to glorify,
> A never dying soul to save,
> And fit it for the sky.
> To serve the present age,
> My calling to fulfill;
> O May it all my powers engage
> To do my Master's Will!

Winston Churchill, between World War I and World War II, when his political fortunes were at an all-consuming low, said "My conviction that the greatest of my work is still to be done is strong within me and I ride reposefully along the gale." At another time he quoted his great ancestor the Duke of Marlborough: "As I think, most things are settled by destiny." Even after having become a world-famous hero for leading Britain to victory in World War II as its prime minister then being voted out of office, he said, "I know I am to be Prime Minister again. I know it." And indeed he was. Author Steven Hayward tells us, "A sense of destiny is often a strong feature of the inner life of great leaders. Destiny does play a genuine role in summoning leadership when it is needed." According to author Loraine Boettner in *The Reformed Doctrine of Predestination*:

> Heroes and conquerors have often been possessed with a sense of destiny which they were to fulfill. This idea of destiny once embraced, as it is the natural effect of the sense of power, so in its turn adds greatly to it. The person as soon as he regards himself as predestined to achieve some great object, acts with so much greater force and constancy for the attainment of it: he is not divided by doubts, or weakened by fears; he believes fully that he shall succeed, and that belief is the greatest assistance to success. The idea of a destiny in a considerable degree fulfills itself.

Each of these comments from history supports the deep, inner sense shared by most of us that we were made for a reason, a very distinct reason, and we were given a destiny to fulfill. Think about the power you could have with such a belief system. What would you do if you knew you could not fail? How well could you perform if you truly believed that what you were doing was something you were supposed to do? This, in fact, is the common denominator among all the greats of history. They felt drawn into the events of their times. They felt created for the very hour they stood on the stage and played their parts. In a word, they felt destined.

William H. Murray said, "The moment one definitely commits oneself, then Providence moves too. All sorts of things occur to help one that would never otherwise have occurred. A whole stream of events issue from the decision, raising in one's favor all manner of unforeseen incidents and meetings and material assistance which no man could have dreamed would come his way." Talk about possibility thinking! It's the "Providence moves too" concept that we are examining here. What could be more motivating than to know that what you are doing is destined, that you are supposed to do it, and that Providence moves to help you?

Destiny is the deepest level of motivation available. Understanding it can be the most motivating, stimulating, sustaining force on your life's efforts. Respect it, nourish it, meditate on it, pray about it, and pursue it. After all, it's your destiny! May you live to fulfill it every day!

Legacy

Benjamin Franklin wrote, "If you would not be forgotten, as soon as you are dead and rotten, either write things worth reading, or do things worth the writing."

Legacy results from understanding our purpose in the bigger picture of our destiny and living it to its fullest. What we have and what we are given are not as important as what we contribute and what we leave behind. Life is short. We are here for merely a moment in time. The Bible teaches, "It is appointed unto men once to die" (Hebrews 9:27), and not one of us can avoid it. And when that time comes, what did our life mean? What did we accomplish? What did we contribute? How will we be remembered? Who will care? When the funeral is over and the relatives are back at the church eating potato salad on rickety tables, what will they be saying?

These are the questions of legacy. Stephen Covey calls this discussion "beginning with the end in mind." What if we lived our lives as if we were going to die? Marcus Aurelius said, "Do not live as though you have a thousand years." And more of us should take that advice.

Legacy is the answer to these questions. Whether what we do is positive, giving, and serving of other people, or destructive, selfish, and hurtful to other people, we will leave a legacy. And it is never too soon nor too late to begin thinking about the legacy being erected with the daily living of our lives. Having an overarching purpose, understanding our personal destiny, and being truthful to it are the best components of a worthy legacy. As one famous quote states, "My life is my message."

The Three Levels of Motivation Reconsidered

There is another way to consider these Three Levels of Motivation. The shallowest motivation would consist of Success, which embodies material rewards and respect from others. The next, deeper level of motivation would be Significance, which embodies destiny and perhaps leaving a legacy. The deepest, most empowering form of motivation would be Obedience and Sacrifice to a God-given vision.

We introduce this delineation to illustrate yet another way the concept of progressive levels of motivation can be described. However, the semantics don't really matter. What does matter is that would-be leaders understand the importance of hunger in its various forms, how to discover it, stoke its flames, and fan it into a blazing inferno. And as any leader will soon discover, real, true, lasting accomplishment comes mostly from the "deeper" levels of motivation. Indeed, a strong sense of purpose, an understanding of personal destiny, and the desire to leave a lasting, positive legacy obedient to God's vision for us are by far the strongest types of motivation. Leaders must cultivate these sources of motivation on a regular basis to fuel performance and sustain it over the long haul.

Every action one takes is either one step closer or one step farther from his or her destiny. Remember, many begin the journey. Very few finish well. It's the *hungry* who make it.

Foundational Quality 2: Hone-able

The definition of *hone* is "to sharpen or smooth with a whetstone or to make more acute, intense, or effective." The second foundational quality of a leader is to be hone-able, to have an attitude that allows intensifying and sharpening.

As the saying goes, "You don't know what you don't know." Additionally, what we do know we gradually forget. So if we don't know what we don't know and we're forgetting what we do know, it would probably be a good idea to continue learning. That way we would at least know something!

The great Socrates stated that if he was the wisest man in Athens it could only be because he alone assumed he didn't have all the answers. The point is that when it comes to learning, we should never assume we have arrived. For a leader there is no completion to education. We need to live like we will die tomorrow and learn like we will live forever. When a leader remains teachable, his or her potential is limitless. With this in mind, there are several roadblocks to learning that a leader must constantly avoid.

Arrogance

Being teachable is as much an attitude as anything else. The "know-it-all" attitude is the death warrant of achievement. In the words of F. A. Hayek, "Nothing is more securely lodged than the ignorance of the experts."

Life is dynamic. Our world is in constant change. Nobody can afford to delude himself with thinking he has it all figured out, no matter who he is or what experience he can claim. Arrogance produces ignorance, and ignorance for a leader is anything but bliss. A true leader knows that no matter how much he has achieved, he still has more to learn.

The opposite of arrogance is humility. To whom is a leader to be humble? The answer: Anyone who has something to teach. Most important, this means being humble toward mentors (more on this in later chapters). Second, it means being humble toward peers, and, finally, it means acting humble toward subordinates. Leaders can learn from anyone in any position and should have a humble attitude that allows learning to take place. Arrogant leaders don't learn until it's too late, if at all.

Disinterest

Being teachable requires energy. That energy comes from the hunger we've previously discussed. In the area of teachability a leader's ambition becomes evident. A leader must be sincerely interested in learning more on a regular basis. Disinterest or apathy will lead to outdated knowledge and poor decision making. Neither of these can exist for long without fatal results in the life of a leader's endeavors.

Wrong Assumptions

A leader may be open and interested in learning but still blinded by wrong assumptions. Sometimes those closest to a situation cannot see something that is obvious to a fresh set of eyes. Leaders must guard against incorrect assumptions. As President Ronald Reagan was fond of saying to Soviet premier Mikhail Gorbachev, "Trust, but verify." Leaders must have open and inquisitive minds and be slow to jump to conclusions based on previous assumptions.

Entrenched Habits

We are all a product of our habits. Habits can be good, and they can be damaging. Habits are our friend when they take us through the

> **Entrenched habits that prohibit the process of learning are poison.**

mundane parts of life as though we were on "auto-pilot." How cumbersome would it be if we had to remember to breathe or get mentally involved in tying our shoes? So many habits are useful. However, what every leader must take care to avoid is leading by habit, never learning anything new, and just doing what he has always done in the manner he has always done it. Such a leader is no longer a leader, but a manager. Entrenched habits that prohibit the process of learning are poison. "That's just the way we've always done it," should never be said by any leader at any time, at any place.

Not-Invented-Here Syndrome

Not-Invented-Here (NIH) syndrome could actually be considered a form of arrogance. When a leader resists learning something new because it wasn't her idea, that leader's educational process is sacrificed on the altar of her pride. Good ideas can and usually do come from everywhere. Great leaders accept and embrace that fact and strive to learn all they can no matter whose idea began the process. Ray Kroc, the founder of McDonald's Corporation, was famous for his enthusiasm for other people's ideas. If a great idea for a burger like the Big Mac was initiated by a certain store in his franchise chain, he would encourage the testing of the idea in that owner's store. If it succeeded, Kroc and his staff would dive into the idea, learn all they could about it, and proceed with implementation across the company. In that way, an enormous corporation could operate on the ideas and innovations of thousands of individuals around the world. A leader should be open to learning about new ideas, no matter the source.

Wrong Priorities

Sometimes a leader may have a healthy attitude about learning but misses the mark by misunderstanding priorities. This usually occurs when the leader is busy doing the wrong things. Leaders must live in the realm of the *important*, not in the realm of the *urgent*. Certainly there are urgent matters that arise on a regular basis in the life of every leader, but if living for the urgent is a chronic condition, the leader will have precious little time to address the important issues. Usually it works like this: A leader begins investing time in important issues, and then gets interrupted by urgent issues. Gradually the urgent issues eat away the time the leader has to spend working on important issues. The more this happens, the more urgent issues erupt, because the important things are not being handled. Eventually the leader is engulfed by urgent crises and has no time for important, vital issues at all.

> *Leaders must live in the realm of the important, not in the realm of the urgent.*

At this point the leader is finished. He has found yet another path from leadership into management. He is no longer leading the flow of events but responding and attempting to manage them. In such a situation, how can a leader have time or energy to learn new things? How could a leader even notice or prioritize what there is to learn? Busy-ness due to wrong priorities is a very common roadblock to the teachability of a leader. Every leader must be aware of this and not let the day-to-day pull of responsibility eclipse his ability to learn and grow.

Cynicism

As with many of these roadblocks to learning, cynicism has much to do with attitude. It can be defined as "the condition of being contemptuously distrustful of human nature and motives." Cynicism is what happens when skepticism is given too much latitude. A small dose of skepticism is healthy in a leader and provides a buffer against gullible mistakes, but if skepticism is allowed to warp a leader's perspective, cynicism is the product.

Leaders approach situations and challenges with a learner's mind-set, that is, as a student and not as a critic. Being judgmental is one of the all-too-common attributes of the unsuccessful who are quick to point out others' flaws or the negative side of a situation. Any fool can find fault, but it takes a winner to find solutions. Or, said another way, losers fix blame while winners fix problems. Leaders must approach learning with a positive, curious inquisitiveness, and never allow their responsibilities or setbacks to sour their dispositions.

A leader must diligently avoid each of the above roadblocks to learning and fight to remain teachable. Learning can be one of life's most rewarding endeavors, and, when applied to the awesome opportunity to grow and flourish as a leader, one of life's biggest blessings. In the case of a leader, though, being teachable goes beyond enjoyment and blessing to being a requirement. To be an unteachable leader is to be a leader headed for a crash.

> *Any fool can find fault, but it takes a winner to find solutions.*

Foundational Quality 3: Honorable

Integrity can be considered as the condition of "not doing what's wrong." Character can be defined as doing the right thing, for the mere reason that it is the right thing, even if that thing is difficult and unpopular. The two sewn together make honor. Author Jeff O'Leary, in *The Centurion Principles*, writes, "'Honor' encompasses the virtues of integrity and honesty, self-denial, loyalty, and a servant's humility to those in authority above as well as a just and merciful heart to those below."

Honor is such a rarely used word in our times that it seems a little old-fashioned. But living a life of integrity and character is timeless and, for a leader, absolutely necessary. It's about choices, and a person's choices in life follow him to the grave.

Is this to say that a person needs to be perfect to become a leader? Of course not. Perfection in this life is not possible, and we, the authors, are certainly not exceptions. However, a leader must strive continually toward perfection even though she knows she can never exactly attain it. It is a question of the heart. The most effective leaders throughout history have led with their hearts, in trust, and with honor. If a leader cuts corners, misuses people, or misrepresents the truth, a time bomb begins ticking. Someday, somewhere, the bomb will go off. It is obvious in our times only too often: public figures at the pinnacle of power and fame crash and burn in a cloud of self-inflicted shame. From political scandals to high-profile corporate frauds, these calamities are brought on by a lack of honor in the leadership.

> *"Human happiness and moral duty are inseparably connected."*

The difference between leaders we revile and those we praise is their individual level of honor. In fact, honor is the force that holds a leader's hunger in check. Without honor, hunger runs rampant and ultimately serves only selfish interests. Honor is the component that makes hunger productive for the leader's fellow man. In fact, what we are basically describing here is another "old-fashioned" word: duty. George Washington said of duty, "Human happiness and moral duty are inseparably connected." So leadership is spawned by hunger and held in check by honor. Under that combination, leaders will find happiness in the fulfillment of their duty to others.

It has been said that the character of a man is the only thing that will walk back from the grave into the hearts of the people who knew him. That is the legacy of a leader. The words a leader says and the walk a leader walks must match. As the saying goes, "Your word is your worth and your worth is your word." Andy Stanley, author of *The Next Generation Leader*, says, "To become a leader worth following you must give time and attention to the inner man. To leave a legacy that goes beyond accomplishment alone, a leader must devote himself to matters of the heart." Character is developed in the valleys and the peaks of life, enabling a person to overcome obstacles and deal with success. Abraham Lincoln observed, "Nearly all men can handle adversity, but if you really want to test a man's character—give him power." Character connects a person to what is right and true. If reputation is what others think of you, then character is what God knows about you.

This concept of honor is so important to a leader because people will follow a leader only as far as they feel they can trust him. People will not follow a leader they can't trust. According to R. Ruth Barton, "We set young leaders up for a fall if we encourage them to envision what they can do before they consider the kind of person they should be." Warren Bennis tells us, "In the leadership arena, character counts. I am not saying this casually. My convictions about character-based leadership come from years of studies, observations, and interviews with leaders and with the people near them. . . . I've never seen a person derailed from [leadership] positions for lack of technical competence. But I've seen lots of people derailed for lack of judgment and character." And, as Heraclitus said, "Man's character is his fate."

Finally, it should be remembered that a major component of honor is personal courage. Without the courage to do what's right because it's right, regardless of ramifications to self, one is not truly worthy to be called a leader.

Hungry, Hone-able, and Honorable: William Wilberforce "Standing Against Evil"

They were shackled like beasts on their backs against the damp wooden planks, arranged in long rows head to toe. Hundreds were lined up from beam to beam and stem to stern of the rancid ship. African tribal chiefs had snatched them from their villages and sold them in Zanzibar to the European traders who were now transporting them across the infamous "middle passage" across the Atlantic Ocean to the Caribbean. There they would serve as forced labor on the sugar plantations. But they had to survive the journey first, and many would not. The conditions were indescribable. Herman Melville wrote, "Slaves were stowed, heel and point, like logs, and the suffocated and dead were unmanacled, and weeded out from the living every morning." Slave ships matching this description had plied back and forth across the Atlantic Ocean for hundreds of years.

Such a hopeless, undignified violation of all that is decent to the instincts of humanity is hard to imagine today. Lord Brougham, a contemporary and avid enemy of the slave trade, called it "the worst of all crimes ever perpetrated by man." How could such a terrible institution be eliminated? Who could wield enough force to abolish it? More importantly, who *would*? From the parched lips of those poor souls transported across the ocean in dark hopelessness, the call for a leader was heard.

In his personal diary on October 28, 1787, an unknown twenty-eight-year-old Englishman answered that call. He wrote, "God Almighty has set before me two great objects, the suppression of the Slave Trade and the reformation of [morals]." In *Character Counts*, author J. Douglas Holladay wrote, "An indefatigable reformer and supreme abolisher of Britain's odious slave trade, Wilberforce arguably led the single most effective stand against evil and injustice in all history." Wilberforce and his followers wrote books and pamphlets, gave speeches, and worked from inside Parliament to illuminate the barbarity of the African slave trade. They persisted year after year in keeping the realities of the practice in the forefront of public discourse.

William Wilberforce would labor for over forty-seven years to see his vision of an abolished slave trade come true, destroying his own health, political career (many had fingered him as a future prime minister), and contemporary reputation. Biographer John Pollock describes Wilberforce's struggle: "The fight was indeed costly and long. Twice Wilberforce was waylaid and assaulted. Certainly he became the most vilified man in England. To make matters worse, Wilberforce was opposed by some of England's greatest heroes and most powerful forces, including the royal family, most of the cabinet, and powerful vested interests." A friend once wrote him saying, "I shall expect to read of you being carbonadoed by West Indian planters, barbecued by African merchants and eaten by Guinea captains, but do not be daunted, for—I will write your epitaph!"

Spurned by the enormity of their calling, Wilberforce and his band of "Saints" (as their enemies mockingly called them), continued throughout their lives to apply pressure on British society and government. England was especially important in the elimination of the slave trade because its navy was the only force in the world capable of stopping the extremely profitable enterprise. Even though slavery in England had been outlawed in 1722, it still thrived throughout other parts of the empire and other countries. Eventually, through the efforts of Wilberforce and those he led, the tide of popular opinion shifted.

As early as 1819 the British navy began forcefully intercepting slave ships on the open seas and setting their captives free. In 1833, just three days before Wilberforce's death, the English Parliament outlawed the slave trade in all its possessions, including the West Indies. The British navy even began enforcing the ban on the slave trade on all other nations, seizing ships and condemning them for carrying even the implements of the slave trade onboard. The American government then began searching its own ships, and eventually, under the administration of Abraham Lincoln, agreed to allow the English to search any American vessel suspected of "slaving." In *To Rule the Waves* Arthur Herman wrote, "The last open slave market in the Americas, at Havana, was finally closed down in 1869, thanks again to British pressure. By then, the British navy was shutting down the slave trade along Africa's eastern coast as well." The African slave trade was dead.

If ever there was an example of a leader possessing the proper foundational qualities of leadership, it was William Wilberforce. He was teachable and eager to learn whatever would serve him in his calling, ambitious beyond reason, and thoroughly a man of character. J. Douglas Holladay outlined some of Wilberforce's foundational qualities:

> Wilberforce and his colleagues were motivated by a robust personal belief in a living God who is concerned with individual human lives, justice, and the transformation of societies. At their core was a profound sense of the presence and power of God, giving them vision, courage, and the necessary perspective to choose their issues and stand against the powerful interests aligned against them. Wilberforce had a deep sense of calling . . . [and] was committed to the strategic importance of a band of like-minded friends devoted to working together in chosen ventures . . . and believed deeply in the power of ideas and moral beliefs.

William Wilberforce stands as a prime example that leaders must be armed with a *deep sense of motivation, indeed, even a calling* that propels them forward through the inevitable challenges that will come their way, even if those challenges present physical danger and come from the "highest born" in the land. (*A leader must be hungry.*)

The measure of a leader's character is primary in influencing other people, as Wilberforce's lifelong diatribe against the immorality of slavery demonstrates. His actions would have carried no weight at all if Wilberforce's own morality had not been beyond reproach. (*A leader must be honorable.*) The height of Wilberforce's honor, the depth of his calling, and the commitment of his energies to learning and working undergirded his leadership. (*A leader must be hone-able.*) The cries of the oppressed were finally answered.

Summary

The three foundational qualities of a leader, the Three Hs, are required to gain access to leadership capability. Being hungry, hone-able, and honorable are required to open the door to the base of the stairs of leadership success.

WHAT A LEADER DOES

CHAPTER 3

The Cycle of Achievement

What counts is not the number of hours you put in, but how much you put in the hours.

—ANONYMOUS

With the foundational qualities in place, the leadership-development process can begin. According to Bill George in *Authentic Leadership*, "Although we may be born with leadership potential, all of us have to develop ourselves to become good leaders."

The leadership-development process is where a leader begins the work that he or she is about and uses that experience to gain ability and understanding. It is this work that propels the leader up the ascending levels of influence. This

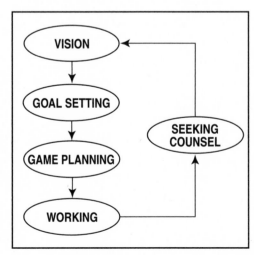

occurs according to the Cycle of Achievement, as shown in the diagram on page 57.

As George Barna, author of *A Fish Out of Water,* said, "Leaders do the right things for the right reasons at the right times." This is not as easy as it may sound. To become capable of such performance, leaders must evolve, and they must do so deliberately. Repeatedly rotating through the Cycle of Achievement compels the leader to grow in ability, understanding, experience, discernment, and wisdom.

Vision

The entire Cycle of Achievement begins with vision. Vision is tomorrow's reality expressed as an idea today. Leaders must first

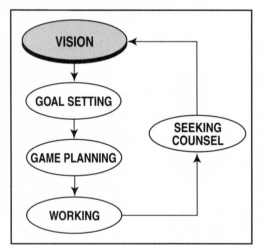

have a vision of where they desire to take themselves and their organization. Kouzes and Posner write, "Leaders inspire a shared vision. They gaze across the horizon of time, imagining the attractive opportunities that are in store when they and their constituents arrive at a distant destination. Leaders have a desire to make something happen, to change the way things are, to create something that no one else has ever created before. In some ways, leaders live their lives backwards. They see pictures in their mind's eye of what the results will look like even before they've started their project, much as an architect draws a blueprint or an engineer builds a model."

Next, leaders must cast the vision consistently before the people they influence. George Barna wrote, "The only way leaders can get their groups to sustain their energy over the long haul is to give them a vision that justifies a long-term commitment. Effective leaders enable people to own the vision as if they had thought it up by themselves and clarify how the individual's gifts and abilities will contribute to making the vision a special legacy. Vision, then, is a portrait of a better future that we may participate in developing."

Vision comes from the picture of a dream in the leader's mind. One doesn't always get what one wants, and one doesn't always get what one deserves, but one *does* generally get what one *pictures*. Having a clear mental picture is the vision the leader carries and casts. Some call it visualization. This is where the dream-building exercise can come in handy, serving to build and maintain a clear vision in the mind of the leader.

Visualization is a technique used across industries and in the sporting world. Motor sports racers and downhill skiers can often be seen moments before a race sitting with their eyes closed, moving their hands back and forth as they imagine themselves racing through the course. They are prerunning the race in their minds, visualizing a perfect performance. In much this same way, leaders in any endeavor must be able to see a future outcome before it can be seen by others. Leaders see farther than others see, and then set about the process of leading them there.

> *One doesn't always get what one wants, and one doesn't always get what one deserves, but one does generally get what one pictures.*

When Walt Disney was nearing death, someone remarked that it was a shame he would not live to see his dream of Disneyland come to fruition. Disney's wife replied that if he hadn't already seen it, it would never have even begun. He had already seen it all in his mind. That's the vision of a leader. That's visualization.

The Bible says, "Where there is no vision, the people perish" (Proverbs 29:18). Leaders supply that vision as the first step in their influence.

Goal Setting

It is important to be hungry and have ambition to change the status quo, with a clear vision of what is to be, but that energy must be directed at something specific. That is where goals enter the picture. David Schwartz, author of *The Magic of Thinking Big*, writes, "A goal is more than a dream; it's a dream being acted upon." In the words of hockey great Wayne Gretzky, "You will miss 100% of the shots you don't take." We must assume he was referring to shots on a *goal*. Without specific goals at which to direct energies and ambitions, all efforts will be wandering generalities at best. Henry David Thoreau wrote, "It is not enough to be busy, so too are the ants. The question is: what are we busy about?" A leader must know the goal of his or her efforts. A leader must know clearly what is to be achieved. In short, leaders use the process of goal setting.

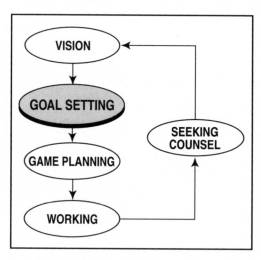

The story is told of two men who set out to accomplish similar results. One invested the effort to set goals properly and the other did not. At the end of a period of time, both men had worked diligently, but the one who had set a specific goal by far outperformed the other man. This is because everything the goal-setting man did was unconsciously directed toward his goal. If there was something to be done, it was first determined if it would assist him in accomplishing his goal. If it would, then he did it. If it would not help him hit his goal, he would not do it. You see, the goal-setting man had the advantage of priorities over the non-goal-setting man. He also had the advantage of channeling his efforts more effectively through the power of focus. On any given day there are a number of "good" things to be done, but there are only a few "great" things to be done. And there can be only one "best" thing to do. A leader knows and does the "best" things on a regular basis.

Like with hunger, goal setting is a discipline. It should never be a haphazard affair. As Tom Garriga, president of Tang Wei Martial Arts Institute, tells us, "A goal is an enemy to be conquered with a battle strategy and the commitment of a warrior. The leadership process is founded on resolve and commitment." With this in mind, there are several components to the proper setting of goals that every leader should embody.

Goals Must Be Specific

Goals must be clear and exact. A leader cannot passionately pursue a generality. Examples of proper specific goals would be, "to win the Boston Marathon," or "to become president of the company," or "to sell one million dollars' worth of products this year." These are clear and precise. Examples of goals that may not be specific enough are "to become a better father," or "to improve in leadership ability," or "to maximize performance at work." These are general feelings of what could be accomplished, but terms like "better father" or "improve ability" or "maximize" are not specific enough to trap the leader into performing. Loose terms like these provide "wiggle room" for the leader. How can one know if he really became a better father or improved his ability or maximized? Being specific with goals not only gives the leader a clear target at which to shoot, but it also leaves no room for doubt as to whether the target was hit. That is what it means to be specific.

Goals Must Be Written

A goal is not a goal until the leader has written it down. This may sound trite, but it is vitally important. As with goals that are not specific, goals not written down leave the leader room to maneuver if things don't go as planned. But a written goal is hard to avoid.

Goals Must Be Set in Stone

The purpose of having a goal in the first place is to organize a leader's thoughts and provide something specific for which to strive. The setting of a goal must be backed by commitment, or the whole process breaks down. Therefore, goals must be "set in stone." Once decided upon, goals should not be changed. There is a saying, "Goals are etched in stone, but plans are drawn in sand." As will be shown in "Game Planning," it may be necessary to modify plans for how to attain a goal, but the goal itself must remain firm. Commitment says that whether the goal is accomplished using Plan A or Plan Z, the goal remains.

Goals Must Be Measurable

If a goal is to exert a motivating force upon the leader, then there must be a clear, quantifiable method to determine when the goal is accomplished. Can it be measured? How? How easily, and by whom? How quickly upon completion? These are the types of questions to answer when setting a goal to ensure that the leader knows when and how a goal is achieved. The ability to measure progress toward a goal also enables mid-course corrections and the ability for a leader to confront brutal reality concerning his or her progress.

In sports, there is nearly always a scoreboard that is big and obvious to all contenders and fans alike. It is present all the time with a constant, specific, measurable update on how the participants are performing toward the goal of winning. Goals for leaders must be just as clear and measurable.

Goals Must Be Realistic

A leader is not a leader without a vision for a better reality, but in the area of goal setting this can be taken too far. It is one thing to have a big vision for a better future reality, and it is okay for that vision to seem wild and crazy to anyone except the leader, but the proper way to use goal setting to accomplish that enormous vision is through gradual steps. Each of these steps is represented by realistic, attainable goals. If the goal is too far beyond the leader's reach, the leader will eventually become exasperated at his repeated failure to accomplish that goal. Goals must be realistic enough that the leader believes them achievable and is energized to do whatever it takes to accomplish them.

Goals Must Provide Motivation

On one hand, goals must be realistic, but on the other, they must be enough of a stretch to inspire the leader. They must be challenging. They must cause discomfort on the part of the leader and provide an impetus for increased performance. The best way to set a goal is to make sure it is between the ditches of "too enormous" on one side and "too easy" on the other. The leader must believe that he or she can accomplish the goal, while at the same time be uncomfortable at the increased level of performance required to do so.

Goals Must Be in Line With Priorities and Values

In the struggle for achievement, there will always be temptations to "sell out" or compromise one's beliefs. There may be conflicts of interest that crop up along the way, but under no circumstances whatsoever should a leader set goals that don't ring true with her true priorities and values in life. As the verse says, "For what shall it

> *A goal forgotten is a goal missed.*

profit a man, if he shall gain the whole world, and lose his own soul?" (Mark 8:36). Every leader should take care when setting goals to ensure that the goal itself is not at cross-purposes with her core beliefs, nor that what's required to accomplish the goal compromises her honor.

Goals Must Be Prominent

The leader must develop systematic ways of regularly reminding himself of the goal. This can be done with signs or placards placed around the home or workplace or even in the car. This may mean telling a spouse or friend or work associate about the goal so he can continue to bring it up in conversation. (This step should be done cautiously, however. The Bible warns against "casting your pearls before swine," [Matthew 7:6], which means be careful with whom you share your most cherished thoughts, including personal goals. Sharing of goals should be done only with the closest of trusted individuals.) Certain music or thoughts can trigger a leader to focus time and again on the goal. The point is that a leader should devise methods of keeping the goal prevalent and in view until the goal is achieved. A goal forgotten is a goal missed. Great leaders know to put pressure on themselves by developing creative reminders of their commitments to achievement.

Goals Must Have a Specific Time Period

Once a leader sets a specific goal, writes it down, commits to it, determines how to measure it, makes sure that it is realistic and motivational and in line with priorities and values, and devises methods for making it prominent, it is crucial that an appropriate time limit be determined. If a goal is set without a time limit, it becomes nothing more than a wish or fantasy. A time limit applies the final pressure on the leader, like a clock ticking during the running of a race. Motorcycle racers say, "When the gate drops, the talk stops." That's how it is with goals once a deadline has been established. A leader bolts from the starting line headed toward the goal and racing against the clock. The pressure of the clock is necessary to avoid the old saying, "When all is said and done, there is usually more said than done!"

Game Planning

With these nine details of goal setting in place, the leader is focused, supercharged, and ready to perform. Almost.

Referencing the Cycle of Achievement diagram once again, we see that there is another step before the work begins that ensures that the work leads directly to the accomplishment of the goal: formulating a game plan. A leader with a goal but no game plan is like an archer with a target and no arrows. A game plan is a leader's strategy or map. It provides guidance toward 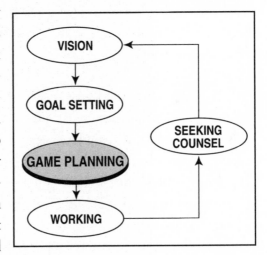 the goal. It provides the very way to realize the goal. It is here that the leader's creative powers can flourish. It is here that a leader develops the ability to think strategically, brainstorming on the methods of attack. It is here that experience and learning can be big enablers. If Hunger provides the "why," the Goal is the "what," and the Game Plan is the "how."

Game Plans Are Set in Sand

Strategic thinking is important, and putting together a well-thought-out plan for accomplishing a goal is vital. But a leader must never allow the game plan to become a masterpiece of its own. The game plan must be fluid, adaptable to changing conditions, and able to be scrapped at a moment's notice if it's not working. No plan entirely survives its collision with reality. As mentioned above, often it is necessary for a leader to develop multiple game plans over time before a goal can be reached. The goal is set in stone; the plan is drawn in sand.

Game Plans Drive the Prioritization of Tasks

One of the biggest advantages of a game plan is that it drives the process of setting priorities. A leader must think through and understand the question, What's important next?

A teacher sought to demonstrate for his students the impact of prioritizing work. He took a glass jar and placed it on the desk next to some large rocks, some smaller rocks, some pebbles, some sand, and a pitcher of water. He informed the class that the object of the exercise was to fit as many of the materials on the desk into the glass jar as possible, providing the densest combination. He first placed as many of the large rocks into the glass jar as would fit, asking the class to confirm that the jar was "full." Next he placed the smaller rocks into the jar around the larger rocks until the class verified once again that no more rocks could be placed into the jar. Then he crammed the pebbles into the jar around the other rocks until no more would fit. Next he poured the sand around the various-sized rocks until no more would go into the jar. Finally he poured the pitcher of water into the sand in the jar until the jar was entirely full of matter and not one more thing would fit.

"Now the jar is full," said the teacher. "If we had not prioritized what should be placed first into the jar, we would not have fit as many of the items into the jar, and we would not have obtained the densest result."

"I don't get it," said a student. "How does that teach priorities?"

"Because," answered the patient instructor, "if we had started with the smaller items such as water or sand, there would have been no room for the bigger-size rocks. The projects we encounter in life must be handled in the same way. Put the big rocks in first, then work downward toward the smaller things."

That is the lesson of priorities. Game planning for a leader is the step where this takes place. Without it, the leader will spend time on things that are "good" to do or even "great" to do, but not the "best" to do. A leader knows to put in the big rocks first.

> *A leader knows to put in the "big rocks" first.*

Ed Koch, author of *The 80/20 Principle*, writes, "The 80/20 Principle asserts that a minority of causes, inputs, or effort usually lead to a majority of the results, outputs, or rewards. Taken literally, this means that, for example, 80 percent of what you achieve in your job comes from 20 percent of the time spent. Thus for all practical purposes, four-fifths of the effort—a dominant part of it—is largely irrelevant." Over time, the leader's ability in this area compounds toward excellence or devolves toward mediocrity. Remember, a leader is most valuable where she adds the most value. Andy Stanley, author of *The Next Generation Leader*, wrote, "The ability to identify and focus on the few necessary things is a hallmark of great leadership."

Game Plans Are Developed at the Macro, Mini, and Micro Levels

A close relative to the topic of prioritization is the classification of tasks or objectives into different levels based upon their size or importance. It is helpful for a leader to understand that issues can be classified into at least three categories. These are:

1. Macro
2. Mini
3. Micro.

The Macro level is the overall top layer. It is comprised of all the big stuff, the high-priority stuff, or the issues that will have the biggest impact for a given task. The Mini level is just below Macro, where issues are smaller and not quite as important. Finally, the Micro level is the tiniest, detail level where the issues are the smallest.

It is important to understand how Macro, Mini, and Micro fit together with the idea of priorities discussed above. The diagram below shows how a leader has a set of priorities that are arranged according to the principle of "What's important next." Associated

PRIORITIES

ISSUES	HIGH	MEDIUM	LOW
MACRO	MOST IMPORTANT		
MINI			
MICRO			LEAST IMPORTANT

with each of these priorities are macro, mini, and micro issues. These two concepts together show the leader exactly where to focus to have the highest impact on reaching the goal. A truly effective leader structures a game plan that starts with the highest-priority task and the macro issues associated with that task. As these are completed the leader works on the next lower-priority tasks and on issues related to those tasks that go from macro down to micro.

It should be noted that this chart is only one way to classify the work a leader must accomplish. It is rarely necessary that all the priorities be handled or all the issues worked out. Often a goal can be reached before that level of detail is necessary. For this reason it is important for leaders to review their priorities and issues continually, to have the highest impact possible as conditions change and progress is made.

Game Plans Are Best When Effective Thinking Is Used First

A leader's quality of thinking will have much to do with that leader's success. There is a tremendous power in effectively thinking through a goal and how it might be attained.

Brainstorming is the process where thinking is done in a freewheeling style, omitting any early judgments as to the merits of the ideas that result. Evaluation of ideas can come later. Brainstorming is designed to pull all good ideas out of the head and into the game plan.

Napoleon Hill became famous for his landmark book, *Think and Grow Rich*. His basic premise was that each of us holds true wealth in the power of our thoughts. The Bible says, "For as a man thinketh in his heart, so is he" (Proverbs 23:7). Dennis Waitley, former Blue Angels pilot and successful author and speaker, said that we have entered in our times a "battle of the mind." We are no longer in the Industrial Age, but in the Information Age. And it really won't be quality of information, but quality of interpreting that information, that will make the difference.

A key precept to comprehend when thinking strategically through a goal can be understood by envisioning the process like a game of dominoes. For any given goal there are myriad tasks that lead to its accomplishment. When drawing up a game plan, the leader must ask, "What are the major dominoes that will knock all the others down?" It is critical to focus on the major tasks first. This requires forethought and planning. Once a leader has determined the steps of major importance toward the realization of a goal, all efforts should be brought to bear on the completion of those particular steps. This happens before becoming involved in lesser concerns. It is these "majors" that leaders are chiefly responsible for accomplishing. They are entrusted to no one else. Often people miss this point and spend time and energy working on dominoes that don't knock any others down. At the end of the time frame, the goals have gone unaccomplished and the leader is frustrated. Effective thinking leads to a proper game plan that prevents this common mistake.

Working

With goals set and game plans made, the leader must exert as much influence as possible toward their achievement. This is not done in a vacuum. The very definition of a leader says that other people are involved. This means that the job of the leader may seem a little less straightforward than the jobs of his subordinates. This section is designed to teach the mind-sets and attitudes of the leader's endeavors, not the details of the actual work to be done. It is meant to be as broad as possible so that leaders of all fields will find relevance for their own situations.

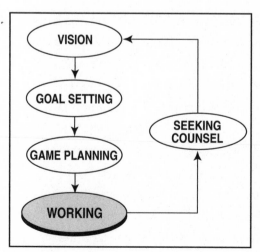

When applied to a leader, the term *working* encompasses several categories. Each of these is necessary in the daily actions of a leader to produce effectiveness. People will work a lot harder when they understand how their efforts fit into the bigger picture.

Working: Casting the Vision

The whole Cycle of Achievement begins with the vision of the leader, as has already been discussed. That vision must be cast and recast before the organization to make sure everybody is working in unison and understands the overall picture. People need to understand how their efforts fit into the bigger picture; it has been proven that people are much more motivated by purpose and cause than anything else. It falls to the leader, then, to be the amplifier and consistent reminder of the organization's vision.

Leadership expert and author George Barna said, "In most of the ministries and businesses for whom I have consulted, followers have no gripe with the vision—they simply have no sense of personal participation in its pursuit. Great leaders help individuals find their roles in pursuing the vision."

Working: Leading by Example

Abraham Lincoln said, "Example is not the main thing in influencing other people; it's the only thing." First and foremost, the leader sets the example. "What you do speaks so loudly that what you say I cannot hear," points directly to the heart of the matter. Many seem to have the idea that a leader is someone with a position, or someone with the ability to talk a good game. But a true leader sets the example with his or her actions on a daily basis, period.

In the movie *We Were Soldiers*, Mel Gibson plays the part of real-life Lt. Col. Hal Moore, a grizzly leader committed to his troops. In one of the first major engagements of the Vietnam War, fought in the Ia Drang Valley, Moore fulfills his promise to his men that he would be the first one off the helicopter and the last man to leave at the end of the battle. After heartbreaking tragedy and unimaginably difficult battle situations, Hal Moore and his troops finally repel the enemy and are cleared for evacuation. As the last helicopter lifts off, Hal Moore finally steps aboard, the last man to leave the battlefield, as promised. He was there for every moment of the battle with them, a leader by example.

Working: Demonstrating a Strong Work Ethic

There is no shortcut to success. Leaders who search for a short-cut end up getting cut short. Although hard work is not the sole secret to success, it is certainly a critical component. Sometimes those in a position of leadership want to shirk the grunt work and instead tell others what to do, but that is not true leadership. When a leader resorts to delegating because he is not willing to do it himself, he has reverted to managing instead of leading. True leadership is being willing to live down in the trenches where the action is and do whatever is necessary.

> *"Courage to act defines the leader."*

Please don't misunderstand us here. A leader's job is not to tackle the tasks and responsibilities of his subordinates. A leader must simply be willing to, as there is no job below the leader. Peter Drucker said, "No leader is worth his salt who won't set up chairs."

More importantly, though, a leader must be willing to exert himself in his own specific duties, not expecting success to come easily or cheaply. The Bible says, "If any would not work, neither should he eat" (Thessalonians 3:10). When asked about the hard work involved in conducting successful scientific experiments, the great inventor Thomas Edison said, "Nothing that's good works by itself, just to please you. You've got to *make* the . . . thing work."

It's going to take work to become a successful leader—plain

and simple. But one shouldn't despair; meaningful work can be one of life's biggest blessings. The strong work ethic demonstrated by the leader energizes the organization and propels everyone forward. As Andy Stanley said, "Courage to act defines the leader."

Working: Taking Responsibility

Leaders take responsibility for their actions and for their decisions. Leaders are not always right and don't always make the right decisions. Real leaders make decisions, and then they make those decisions right.

Al Kaltman says, "The successful [leader] gets superior performance from ordinary people." That happens because the leader takes responsibility for those results. A leader does not make excuses. A leader does not place blame on others. A leader does not evade duty. Kaltman continues, saying, "Good [leaders] realize that they alone are ultimately responsible for the success or failure of their efforts. They do not establish alibis or look to lay blame on others."

> If you're talking about your effort, then your results must be poor.

Taking responsibility means holding oneself to a standard of results. Leaders are not satisfied with being busy, or with talking an issue to death. True leaders are only happy with outcomes. As the old saying goes: "If you're talking about your *effort*, then your *results* must be poor." If leaders don't like the outcomes, they make changes, taking full responsibility for implementing those changes. If something goes wrong, they take the blame. If something goes well, they share the credit. But underneath it all, the leader takes ownership and determines that "If it's to be, it's up to me!"

President Harry Truman was known for his straightforward thinking and no-nonsense approach to decision making. As a young man after World War I, Truman opened up a haberdashery with a war buddy. The business went bankrupt, but Truman accepted responsibility and paid back all the debts. Later in life, as president, Harry Truman had a sign on his desk that read, "The buck stops here." Truman understood that along with leadership comes the responsibility to make tough decisions.

Truman had been vice-president for only eighty-two days and had not been informed on the major issues facing the president when President Franklin Roosevelt passed away. Harry Truman was thrust into the middle of World War II as the leader of the United States and asked to make monumental decisions without the luxury of time for studying the major issues. This is where Truman's ability to make tough choices paid off. When faced with issues like the use of the atomic bomb, communist intervention in Greece, the Korean conflict, and power struggles with General MacArthur, Truman thrived and accepted the responsibility that came with leadership. The old saying "When in command, take charge" seemed to fit President Truman aptly.

Accepting responsibility is one of the essential traits of every leader. In fact, the greatness of a leader is directly proportional to the amount of responsibility accepted and handled. For President Truman, everything began and ended with taking responsibility for his actions and decisions, placing blame nowhere but with himself.

Leaders take responsibility, period.

Working: Orchestrating and Aligning Resources

A true leader assumes responsibility for orchestrating and aligning resources. This involves equipping others or making sure that others are adequately managing resources. The best leadership team in the world cannot function if it runs out of what it requires to operate.

Many are the stories of leaders whose grand visions failed because of a lack of resources or proper allocation thereof.

Napoleon's Grand Army marched against Russia and got trapped by winter and a total lack of resupply. As the French forces advanced, the Russian forces burned and destroyed every scrap of food or crop that could be used by Napoleon's troops. As a result, an army of nearly one million men disintegrated. It wasn't a lack of ability or training, nor was it a lack of a strong vision or charismatic leadership; it was a failing of resources. Leaders take full responsibility for the even operation of their organizations and its flow of necessary resources.

Working: Solving Problems and Removing Obstacles

Leaders anticipate problems or obstacles that will impede plans so they can be solved and removed before negative consequences result. This requires active mental engagement. Leaders must constantly be thinking and searching for anything that will crop up to bring catastrophe to their operations. When these things are identified, or even suspected, strategic plans must be put in place to eradicate them. The best way to deal with a problem is to attack while the problem is still small. There is no sense in chopping down a full-grown tree later when it could be plucked out as a twig today.

There are two sources of obstacles to the success of a leader's organization. The first is internal elements, and the second is outside influences. Internal obstacles are under the authority of the leader and can be addressed head-on. Fixing these requires courage, healthy confrontation, and firm fairness. External elements may or may not be changeable by the leader, but the leader must find a way to deal with the situation. Leaders who ignore outside interferences or simply hope they will eventually go away are dooming their organization to certain failure. Remember, leaders take responsibility for results. That includes results that are affected by outside factors such as the economy, the actions of a competitor, attack from special-interest groups, weather, and changes in the law. While a leader may not be able to *change* the conditions, he or she is responsible for success *in spite* of those conditions. This requires constant vigilance, strategic and creative thinking, and boldness. Will Durant tells us, "Freedom requires eternal vigilance. Love peace, but keep your powder dry." Leaders in any field would be wise to heed this advice. Success requires constant watchfulness. Harmony and peaceful operating conditions are wonderful, but real leaders know that such conditions are temporary, and they remain on the lookout for the next battle to protect their operation's effectiveness. And we can be certain the next battle is always looming on the horizon. Leaders stand at the ready.

Working: Searching for Opportunities

Leaders have watchful eyes. They scan their world for emerging opportunities all the time. Again, both internally and externally, opportunities crop up on a regular basis. It is the job of the leader to seek and identify these chances and help the organization take advantage of them. This is where the ability to assess and take risks and the ability to prioritize become critical. It is imperative that organizations take advantage of new opportunities, but not every opportunity. Having a clear vision for the operation and understanding its mission form the basis for evaluating new possibilities. If an opportunity is in line with the vision, then leaders take their organizations in that direction—all other possibilities must be left aside. It is the job of the leader to identify, analyze, and decide which opportunities to exploit and which to ignore, all the while casting and recasting the vision so the organization accepts the new challenges with wholeheartedness.

Working: Being Consistent

Since the actions of a leader are the example for the organization, consistency of temperament and performance is a must.

Leaders must be who they are on a constant basis. They must be steady and stabilizing to the organization. They must always be out in front, performing.

We have all watched sports teams who seem to be on fire one week, defeating some great rival, but collapse the next week to an apparently inferior team. We know that teams exhibiting this behavior will not have championship seasons. It is the same in all areas of leadership. Consistency builds confidence among the rank and file. Consistency demonstrates conviction and commitment. When a leader is consistent, he or she demonstrates a maturity that is not only admirable, but duplicates throughout the organization.

Remember, followers emulate the behavior of the leader. One test of a leader's consistency is the performance of the organization. If it is erratic and unpredictable, that may say something about the leader's consistency, or lack thereof.

The fable is told of two frogs that fall into a vat of milk, where they struggle to tread and stay afloat. One frog treads furiously, tires himself out, and sinks to the bottom. Then he reemerges only to tread furiously once again. This pattern repeats until eventually he tires himself out and drowns. The other frog treads too, but stays at it consistently, pacing himself and churning constantly. Eventually, that consistency churns the milk into butter and the frog is able to hop out.

Consistency for a leader produces an accumulation of results.

Working: Maintaining Focus

Leadership is largely a game of knowing "what to leave in and what to leave out." For nearly any leader in any position, there will continually be a myriad of attractions and distractions all vying for the leader's attention. True leadership requires the ability to focus.

> **True leadership requires the ability to focus.**

The analogy that comes to mind involves the comparison of a flashlight to a magnifying glass. A flashlight disperses light while a magnifying glass concentrates it. A leader must be like a magnifying glass, focusing all of his or her efforts upon the main points or priorities. Dispersed, a leader's efforts might not accomplish much more than lighting up a sidewalk, but focused, they can fry insects!

Working: Staying Persistent

Success lies on the other side of inconvenience and struggle. To make it through to the rewards, a leader must learn to persist. How many would-be leaders have failed only because they didn't hang in there long enough? Success in many cases means hanging on after everyone else has been shaken off. Samuel Johnson said, "Great works are performed not by strength but by perseverance."

Leaders recognize that they must hang in there and continue the fight even when all seems lost. Many times, victory is just around the corner.

Working: Striving Ahead of the Group

Leaders must lead. That means that they must be out front, demonstrating achievement. Leaders must exert a "pull" on their organizations with the strength of their own performance. This is the opposite of "pushing" an organization. Managers push, leaders pull.

Dwight D. Eisenhower was the commanding general of the Normandy invasion during World War II and the thirty-fourth president of the United States. To explain leadership, Eisenhower was known to reach into his pocket and retrieve a small string. "That piece of string illustrates the main principle of leadership," he would say. "Push the string and you can barely get it to move. But pull the string, and it will follow you anywhere."

Working: *Giving Praise and Recognition*

As discussed in the section on motivation, the desire for recognition is universal. Everybody appreciates a sincere compliment.

Leaders look for ways to compliment their performers. They specialize in catching people in the act of doing things right, and they don't hesitate to lavish praise. All leaders should live by Harry Truman's great words: "You would be surprised at how much you can accomplish when you don't care who gets the credit." Napoleon Bonaparte, famous for his ability to inspire passion in his followers, said, "Men are more easily led by decorations than by authority or force."

Working: *Providing Guidance and Course Correction*

Ultimately a leader acts as a coach. One definition of a coach is "a vehicle that carries you from where you are to where you want to go." While this definition obviously refers to the horse-and-buggy type of coach, it has cross-application to what a sports or business coach does. An effective leader or coach helps people go places they want to go but are unable to reach on their own. To do this, a leader provides guidance and direction. A leader is courageous in confronting issues that need resolving. When followers are off track, the leader gives correction. Learning how to make these corrections without hurting feelings or dampening enthusiasm is the hallmark of a good leader. This will be explored at length in Chapter 9.

Work is the crank that turns the engine in the Cycle of Achievement. A leader must embrace hard work, for all the reasons just discussed. Putting these components together gives the leader productivity toward set goals. Henry Wadsworth Longfellow wrote:

> The heights by great men reached and kept
> Were not attained by sudden flight,

But they, while their companions slept,
Were toiling upward in the night.

Seeking Counsel

Experience is not the best teacher; other people's experience is the best teacher. For this reason, every leader must seek out and find credible mentorship. Without tapping into the experience of others, leaders are forced through a trial-and-error process.

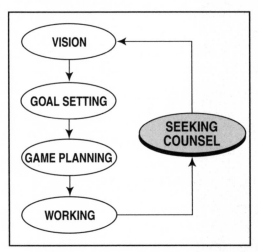

Trial and error is not only painful and frustrating, but it can be extremely time consuming.

Success begins with information from the correct source. Therefore, it is critical that a mentor is chosen based on his or her "fruit on the tree." Receiving mentorship may be done in person with someone interested in sharing his or her wisdom. It may come from studying historical figures with relevance to the undertakings of the leader. Or it may come from studying the materials provided by a speaker or author who can provide wisdom and experience to a leader. By far the best type of mentor, however, is the personally concerned, face-to-face type. Such a mentor is priceless in the career of a leader.

Later in the book we will delve deeper into the concept of mentoring, as every truly great leader must also become a great mentor. At this stage of our study we'll focus on the purposes of seeking counsel from a coach or mentor, the case in which the leader is a protégé to another leader (the mentor).

A Leader Seeks Counsel to Learn

Leaders know they always have more to learn. In fact, the greatest leaders are also the greatest learners. Seeking counsel from qualified sources is one of the most effective ways for a leader to learn. What can a leader learn from mentorship? A leader can gain information, attitudes, perspectives, judgment, strategies, mind-sets, priorities, and objectives. However, this can never occur without humility on the part of the leader. A leader must humble himself before a mentor and agree to take counsel. Author Dennis Rainey asked, "Have you permitted your [mentor] enough access to your life that he or she is able to tell you anything that you need to hear?" Mentors are not there to make leaders feel better or to inflate their egos with unearned praise. Mentors rise above mere friendship and provide needed, straight-ahead guidance. At times this may be uncomfortable for a developing leader, but the price of discomfort with a mentor is much less than the price of discomfort that comes with mistakes in judgment or poor performance in the field.

A cute old saying states, "We have two ears and one mouth. We should use them proportionately." Seeking counsel is a valuable chance for a leader to learn, but it cannot occur unless the protégé listens to what the mentor has to say. Too many times ambitious would-be leaders are more interested in talking than listening. It is okay to want to impress a mentor, it is okay to be enthusiastic about having time with a coach, but listening must be done enthusiastically for any learning to take place.

For a leader, learning is not optional. Learning will come either through study and mentorship or through experience, but learning will come. Smart leaders seek to learn on the "front end" through mentorship, and save the learning that occurs with experience for good experiences.

A Leader Seeks Counsel to Gain Perspective

One of the most valuable things to be gained from a mentor is perspective. Webster defines perspective as "a view of things in their true relationship or importance." How a leader sees things is paramount. Properly defining a problem, with the correct perspective, is by far the biggest component in finding the solution. Often leaders are simply too close to a situation. They struggle with it and fight it but lose the overall perspective that a mentor can provide. Also, in many cases, mentors have had experience in similar situations and can provide historical perspective. Either way, leaders need the insights and perspectives mentors provide. Properly utilized, these perspectives can radically enhance a leader's performance, saving the leader from frustration and wasted time.

A Leader Seeks Counsel to Make Mid-Course Corrections

Even when a leader is clear on the objectives and implements a well-thought-out game plan, things can go awry. Sometimes progress lags behind the plan. When these glitches occur, mentors can provide invaluable insights into changes in the game plan that will still allow for the attainment of the goal.

Picture a person wandering across a great expanse of desert, as shown below:

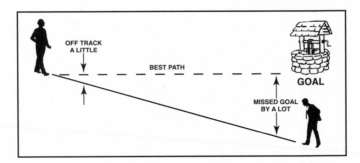

The person's goal is to make it to the well of fresh water several miles in the distance. The wellhead is small and cannot be seen by the traveler, but the traveler knows the general direction in which to walk. Notice how the traveler can get off track just a small amount early in the journey. Notice also how this amplifies throughout the journey to the point where the walker has gone far enough to reach the well, but is still miles away from it. Now let's take a look at another traveler seeking the same fresh water:

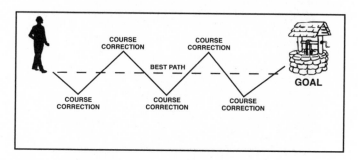

A guide or mentor who has been to the well before accompanies this sojourner. At intervals along the way, the mentor initiates small corrections in direction. At the end of the journey, not only has the mentor saved the traveler a lot of wasted steps, but also has ensured that the traveler makes it to the well and survives to walk another day. And so it is in the life of a leader. Mentors provide these all-important corrections along the way to keep the leader from missing the mark entirely and ending up with disaster.

A Leader Seeks Counsel to Receive Feedback

Just like a student receiving a report card, leaders obtain feedback on their performance from mentors. Leadership can be complicated. In some cases, leaders can become fuzzy-headed regarding their performance. It can be difficult at times to know if progress is being made toward overall objectives. Mentors slice through the confusion and clarify the picture, providing the leader with clear feedback on his or her performance. A mentor can provide a positive outlook, where the leader sees only his own failures. A mentor can also keep the developing leader's head from "swelling" by shining a light on areas for further improvement.

This is where it is a big help if goals have been set correctly and game plans are clear and well structured. Mentors can provide feedback on how well the leader is working according to priorities, on the mind-set and attitude of the leader, and on the leader's progress toward the goals.

A Leader Seeks Counsel to Be Held Accountable for Results

How well did the leader do in reaching his objectives? How did the leader grow in understanding and experience? Is the leader progressing in ability and character? The answers to all these questions, while evaluated by the mentor, are the responsibility of the leader. Remember, leadership is a "the buck stops here" profession. There are no excuses or places to hide. When a leader counsels with a mentor it is time to open up and honestly report results. When those results are lacking for one reason or another, leaders hold themselves accountable to their mentors for improvement. This is sometimes tough. Nobody likes to look bad or fail in front of someone they respect. But leaders must resist the urge to "candy coat" their performance. Instead, leaders must open up and be entirely honest with their mentors. This is no time for a protégée to be concerned with impressing her mentor. It is the time for getting answers. Only with such a system of accountability can true leadership development be optimized.

> *Leaders must grow personally. It is a fact of life for leaders that they have to get better.*

A Leader Seeks Counsel to Grow Personally

The overall goal of mentorship is to grow the leader. It is fine to advance the leader's performance and help the leader hit some goals, but these are just the playing field on which the athlete is strengthened. The real goal is for the leader to experience significant personal growth. Ultimately, there is no sustainable growth in results without growth in the leader. Leaders must grow personally. It is a fact of life for leaders that they have to get better. And they must commit to growing on a regular basis. As the saying goes, the speed of the leader is the speed of the group. Mentors are there to provide guidance and place a continued emphasis on personal growth.

A Leader Seeks Counsel to Earn Respect

To be respected by the respected is every leader's desire. Said another way, to be blessed by the best overcomes all the rest. Money and fame and power and prestige may all have some charm, but there is nothing like earning the respect of someone who has been instrumental in teaching and guiding our own growth and success. Leaders know this about themselves and strive to earn the respect of their mentors.

The Cycle of Achievement: Mel Fisher "Today's the Day"

Spain was the world's dominant superpower, undisputed on land in continental Europe and master of the world's seaborne trade. Each year a massive flotilla of ships would make their way from New World ports in the Caribbean Sea to Madrid with the year's harvest of gold and silver bullion from the mines of Mexico and Peru. The wealth of the "Spanish Main" kept King Philip III ahead of his enemies and funded his enormous military.

On Sunday, September 4, 1622, the Tierra Firme fleet of twenty-eight ships sailed from the port of Havana, Cuba. The fleet was heavily loaded with treasure intended for Spain and its new king, Philip IV. Well into the hurricane season, sailing was becoming more risky every day. Departure had been delayed for weeks as more than 100,000 additional silver coins and over 1,000 additional silver ingots were loaded. Further delays occurred when more silver coins and bars, as well as over 20,000 pesos in gold bars and discs, were placed onboard. The treasure, however, would never arrive.

The very next day a hurricane struck the fleet and eight ships were driven onto a reef in the Florida straits. Chief among these ships was the *Nuestra Señora de Atocha*, which had a 110-by-33-foot hull loaded with treasure. Of 265 people onboard, only five survived to tell the tale. Treasure was scattered over a ten-mile stretch of ocean as another great storm, just days later, blew the wreckage off the reef and broke it into splinters. For centuries, treasure hunters attempted to locate and salvage the missing fortune. Over the course of nearly 363 years, no one succeeded.

Then a World War II veteran and enthusiast of the new sport known as SCUBA diving took a fascination to treasure salvaging. He sold his successful dive shop in California and relocated his family to Florida to search for the *Atocha* and other shipwrecks like her. He had to develop equipment of his own, constantly improving it to meet changing conditions. He had to pioneer search and mapping techniques to cover such a large span of ocean. Years passed without any marked results, and Fisher kept the morale of his crew up by stating emphatically each day, "Today's the day!"

After three years of very expensive and meticulous searching, Mel Fisher discovered that, as the result of a geographical misinterpretation, he was searching in the wrong location altogether. He relocated and soon found an anchor believed to have belonged to the *Atocha*. He also found a gold chain and two bars of gold. At this point, the government put agents on his boats and charged Fisher for the expense. They also demanded that he upgrade the working conditions on his boats. The press heard about the discovery of the anchor and accused Fisher of being a fraud. Experts in the area of treasure salvage said Fisher was just staging his finds to solicit funds for his operation. Competitors hungry for a treasure find of their own swooped onto the scene and started shadowing Fisher's work. But with each new challenge, Fisher continued to innovate and improve his techniques, and he continued extolling his crew with "Today's the day!"

Funds had always been low, and soon this dictated that Fisher sell his home and move his family into a dilapidated house boat. All but one of his original team members quit and returned home, discouraged. Then, at the five-year mark, Fisher and his crew found three silver bars. This time, however, the government simply confiscated it all. Then they canceled his approvals and permits, and one state senator even made an obscene gesture as he pulled away in a government boat with the confiscated silver bars. Fisher's competitors said the silver bars were another fraud. The Florida press made him out to be a criminal. Fisher hired some good lawyers and continued the fight, eventually regaining his permits. All the while he continued upgrading his equipment and techniques and believing each day, leaving the dock, that "Today's the day."

Fisher faced more obstacles when his museum and office, both sharing the interior of an old boat, sank next to the dock. Next, the Securities and Exchange Commission launched an investigation into the stock handling of his company. Meanwhile, other competitors arrived on the scene with intimidation tactics like boat ramming and pointing guns at Fisher and his crew, but Fisher and his team continued and soon found seven cannons, which were analyzed and proven to be from the *Atocha*. Fisher was getting close.

The rules changed when the government decided to take over all treasure salvaging in the state of Florida. Fisher filed a lawsuit that he would eventually win, along with almost 150 lawsuits in all! Then his son, an avid part of Fisher's operation, drowned. One has to wonder how difficult it was for Fisher or anyone else to continue believing that "Today's the day."

Fisher found the *Santa Margarita*, another treasure ship from the same fleet as the *Atocha*, one that had been loaded with gold, silver, copper, indigo, and 13,000 pounds of tobacco. This find brought not only much-needed finances, but also verification of Fisher's methods and equipment. This proved that they were indeed getting close to finding the *Atocha*.

It was at this point that one of Fisher's closest partners turned traitor and "jumped claim," attempting to steal some of the recent *Margarita* treasure.

Then Fisher was diagnosed with cancer.

Finally, though, on July 20, 1985, after *seventeen years* of searching, the radio call came in from one of Fisher's search boats: "Put the charts away. We've hit the mother lode!" The *Nuestra Señora de Atocha* had been found. Among the treasure recovered were 1,041 silver bars weighing 80 pounds each, over 230,000 silver coins, $400 million in gold and silver coins and bars, 3,000 Colombian emeralds, gold chains, artifacts, and jewelry. To date, the *Atocha* is the richest treasure ship ever found. At the time of this writing, treasure is still being recovered from the location on a daily basis! It is an understatement to say that Fisher's persistence and tenacity paid off.

The story of Mel Fisher and the discovery of the *Atocha* is a clear illustration of the Cycle of Achievement. Fisher had a clear vision for what he wanted to accomplish, and he created uncontainable enthusiasm in the hearts of those around him when he talked about the treasure of the *Atocha* and how sure he was that they could find it. Talk about casting a vision! Then he set clear and specific goals and developed an effective game plan of ocean mapping and search techniques to bring the goal to fruition. Fisher then did the work with an incredible attitude, stating "Today's the day" when most would have said "Outta here!" He read and learned everything he could along the way about treasure salvaging and its rapidly developing technology. He consulted document experts in Spain to help with interpretation of old ships' manifests. He befriended many experienced treasure hunters along the Florida coast and involved many in his search, developing a full partnership with one having vastly more experience than himself (Seeking Counsel). And he made adjustments and innovations along the way, constantly improving as he rotated again and again, year after year, through the Cycle of Achievement.

Most leaders will not grapple with issues as numerous or life threatening, nor as heartbreaking, as those that confronted Mel Fisher. But every leader will face an array of challenges and opportunities. Applying the principles of the Cycle of Achievement, as Mel Fisher did, will enable the developing leader to realize his vision gradually and hit his own "mother lode" of success.

Summary

It is the iterative Cycle of Achievement loop that leaders deploy in their planned attack on the status quo. Understanding each of the parts and using it as a road map allows leaders to improve their performance on a continuing basis. The Cycle of Achievement gives leaders one way to describe that improvement process and keeps them 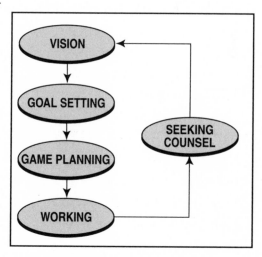 on track as they rotate the cycle over and over again. With every rotation, the leader improves, advances, and betters himself.

HOW A LEADER GROWS PERSONALLY

CHAPTER 4

The Trilateral Leadership Ledger

*I know of no more encouraging fact than the unquestionable
ability of man to elevate his life by conscious endeavor.*

—HENRY DAVID THOREAU

Hugo Grotius was a Dutch lawyer, writer, theologian, and
statesman in the late sixteenth and early seventeenth centuries.
President James Madison called him the "father of the modern
code of nations." On the topic of self-government, Grotius boiled
the idea of leadership all the way down to the level of the individual. He said, "He knows not how to rule a Kingdom, that cannot
manage a Province; nor can he wield a Province, that cannot
order a City; nor he order a City, that knows not how to regulate
a Village; nor he a Village, that cannot guide a Family; nor can
that man Govern well a Family that knows not how to Govern
himself." Authors Mark Beliles and Stephen McDowell simplified
it even further: "You must rule yourself before you rule others."
Too often in our world we see individuals attempting to influence

others when they are barely able to lead themselves. Rich DeVos said, "Before you try to fix the world, clean up your own bedroom." To become a leader, one must gain self-mastery, which can be accomplished only through a program of deliberate personal growth.

Philip Crosby, author of *Quality Is Free*, writes, "There is a theory of human behavior that says people subconsciously retard their own intellectual growth. They come to rely on clichés and habits. Once they reach the age of their own personal comfort with the world, they stop learning and their mind runs on idle for the rest of their days. They may progress organizationally, they may be ambitious and eager, and they may even work night and day. But they learn no more. The bigoted, the narrow-minded, the stubborn, and the perpetually optimistic have all stopped learning."

For leaders, growth cannot be optional. The only way to keep pace with increasing responsibilities is through increased ability. Growth, then, must occur in two categories:

1. Personal
2. Influence with others

This chapter focuses on the first of these, the personal-growth side of leadership development, while the next six chapters will tackle the subject of influence. Personal growth is first, because a leader's ability to influence others stems from his or her personal abilities.

> "Internal victories precede external victories."

Personal growth is *internal*, taking place deep within a leader. Often, when people embark upon the journey of becoming leaders, they feel frustrated at a lack of external results to show for their efforts. But the process of becoming a leader starts with a lot of effort, which results in improvements the outside world cannot yet see. The gains are internal, inside the person. Only later will all the effort at personal growth and improvement show up in the form of external results. Stephen Covey says, "Internal victories precede external victories."

Let us take the building of a skyscraper as an example. The amount of time an architect spends developing the drawings, the time engineers put into designing the main systems, the time to meet with government officials and secure permits, the immense amount of effort involved in digging, pouring, and assembling the foundation, all take place before any results are visible to the casual passerby. Then, once main construction begins, the height of the structure progresses at unbelievable speed. What was once an empty lot is suddenly transformed into an enormous structure. Personal ability and leadership characteristics work the same way.

Because personal growth is internal and the external results show up only much later, we have found it helpful to give leaders a way to self-assess their effectiveness and track their progress. We do this using what we call a Trilateral Leadership Ledger, shown below:

On the left vertical scale of this chart is the ranking of the effectiveness of the leader, with 10 being perfect and 0 being dismal. Across the bottom horizontal scale are the categories of leadership

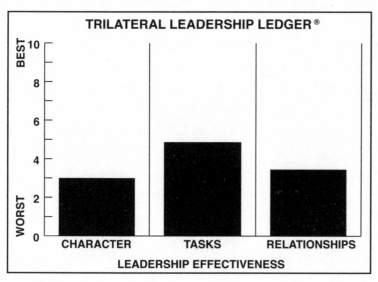

effectiveness. It should be the goal of a leader to grow in the mastery of each of these three areas.

The Three Categories of Personal Effectiveness

Character

We discussed character and the concept of honor in "What a Leader Brings," but it bears further discussion here. We can't emphasize this too much: Nobody lacking character will succeed in a meaningful way.

One of the first things a person on the leadership-development journey should understand is that there is intrinsic value in developing character even if he never obtains external results from his endeavors. This is because who one becomes is much more important than what one accomplishes.

For the purpose of using the Trilateral Leadership Ledger and gauging personal growth, character in this case is considered to include:

1. honesty
2. integrity
3. courage
4. proper values based on absolute truths
5. faith
6. a humble spirit
7. patience with others
8. discipline
9. self-mastery

In *What to Say When You Talk to Your Self*, Shad Helmstetter writes, "Mastering one's future must surely start with managing one's *self*." John MacArthur observes, "Self-control is absolutely vital to lasting success in

> **"Self-control is absolutely vital to lasting success in any endeavor of life."**

any endeavor of life. Many people do attain a degree of prominence on the strength of sheer natural talent alone. But the real, influential leaders are the ones who devote themselves to personal discipline and make the most of their gifts." That is what this category of personal effectiveness is all about.

Tasks

The task category simply represents the ability to get things done. It comprehends all the concepts of "Work" we discussed in the Cycle of Achievement. No leader can succeed without the ability to execute tasks. For assessing a leader's effectiveness and monitoring growth, the task category includes:

1. acceptance of responsibility
2. work ethic
3. availability
4. willingness to invest time
5. tenacity
6. perseverance
7. execution

Yitzhak Rabin, two-time prime minister of Israel and tireless worker for world peace, said of his boyhood, "Our home was permeated with a sense of mission. Work was considered a value in itself." The category of task is the very embodiment of that statement.

Relationships

The category of relationships measures the ability to get along with and form lasting bonds with people. No leader can experience success alone. Such a situation precludes the very concept of leadership. Leaders must accomplish things through, with, and for people, and that can happen only with the ability to build relationships. The relationship category includes:

1. accepting people
2. approving of people
3. appreciating people
4. seeing the good in people
5. encouraging people
6. caring for and about people
7. putting others first
8. seeking win-win arrangements
9. helping people accomplish tasks
10. living the "Golden Rule"

Henry J. Kaiser said, "You seldom accomplish very much by yourself. You must get the assistance of others." That is the focus of the relationship category.

Using the Trilateral Leadership Ledger

A leader can begin the personal growth journey with a self-assessed rating on the Ledger. That will provide a starting point. As the leader progresses using the principles taught in this book, there will be marked improvements, which can then be estimated using the chart. In this way, a leader can keep him- or herself on track and make sure there is not only growth, but growth in all three categories.

Here's how it works. Let's say a certain leader, Mister A., has a fairly high starting score for Character. He estimates himself to be a 4. Next, he knows he is not very task oriented and is prone to procrastination and making excuses, so he rates himself a 1 in the Task category. Finally, Mister A. thinks he is decent at building and sustaining relationships and gives himself a 3 in Relationships. Multiplying the three together gives him a total score of 12. Mister A. uses that as his starting score of Leadership Effectiveness.

One note of caution: In general, people tend to overrate themselves. Often the gap between self-realization and reality is enormous. Recently a survey was taken of managers across the United States. One question on the survey inquired whether or not there was a management crisis in the country. Over two-thirds of the managers responded in agreement that, yes, there was indeed a management crisis. Farther along, the questionnaire asked whether the survey participant was part of the crisis, being a defective manager himself. The majority of respondents answered no; they were not part of the crisis. Two-thirds were certain there was a crisis, and almost all were sure they were not part of its cause!

> *Often the gap between self-realization and reality is enormous.*

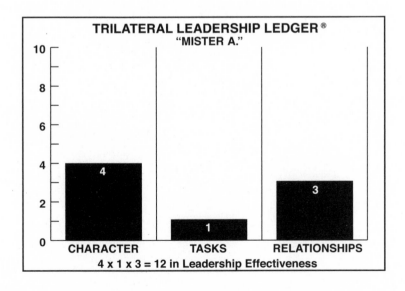

The best use of the Leadership Ledger for someone on the leadership-development journey is to make an honest assessment of his or her starting point. Jim Collins calls it "confronting brutal reality." Asking a mentor's opinion on this self-evaluation may make it more realistic. Only when leaders are courageous enough to face the facts as they really are can they properly size up the challenge and respond appropriately. Leaders can improve only when they decide to improve. And they cannot improve unless they know where they are weak and where they are strong. We don't control where we start our journeys, but we *do* control what we do once we've started. The goal is to take what we've been given and do the most we can with it.

A newer leader will most likely be fairly weak in all categories. Multiplying the numbers together will not result in much of a score. Also, the poorer a leader is in the beginning, the smaller the numbers in each category. That means more effort is required to make an impact on the overall score. For instance, let's say Mister A. improves his ability to build relationships from a 3 where he started to a 4. Recalculating his total score would give him a Leadership Effectiveness of 16, as compared to 12 when he began.

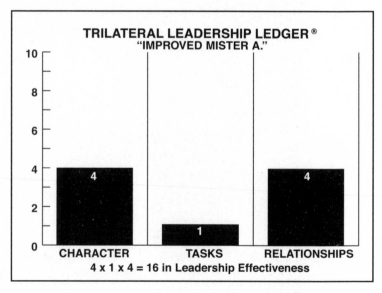

TRILATERAL LEADERSHIP LEDGER ®
"IMPROVED MISTER A."

4 x 1 x 4 = 16 in Leadership Effectiveness

When you consider that perfect Leadership Effectiveness would have a score of 1,000 (10 x 10 x 10), moving from a 12 to a 16 is not very signficant. This is why we say that budding leaders need patience and perseverance. It will take time and effort to improve to the point where external differences can be seen. But by using the Leadership Ledger as a yardstick, Mister A. has moved from a 12 to a 16, which is a 33 percent improvement in his overall Leadership Effectiveness! On a relative basis, that is a huge improvement. The outside world may not be able to tell it yet, but Mister A. is on his way.

We have heard it said that one should focus on his or her strengths and the weaknesses will take care of themselves. In the more lopsided cases, the Leadership Ledger shows this to be false. Let's consider the person who generates decent scores in two categories but a really low one in the remaining category. Mister B. assesses himself with a Character rating of 3, a Tasks rating of 6, and a Relationships rating of 0. Multiplying the numbers together, we can see that no matter how much character Mister B. develops or how many tasks Mister B. accomplishes, he is doomed to have no Leadership Effectiveness because his relationship score is so abysmal, meaning that he is not good at maintaining relationships. Anything times zero is still zero.

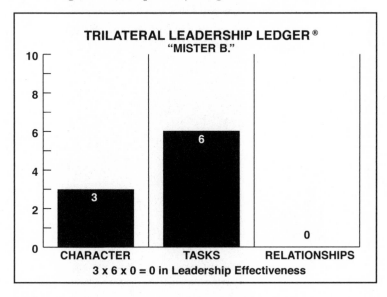

TRILATERAL LEADERSHIP LEDGER ®
"MISTER B."

3 x 6 x 0 = 0 in Leadership Effectiveness

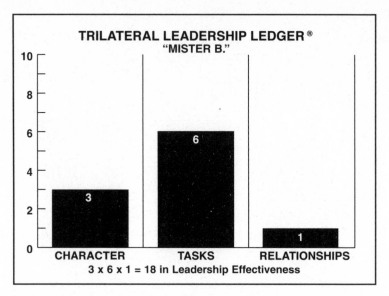

What if Mister B. increases his Relationships to a 1? His over-all Leadership Effectiveness score would still be only 18 out of a possible 1,000.

What if Mister B. improved his strongest area, Tasks, from 6 to 8? That would be an incredible improvement, and an assessment of 8 is really getting up there, but yet it would result in a score of just 24!

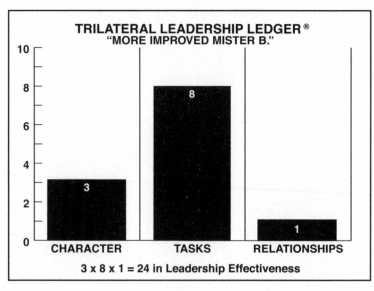

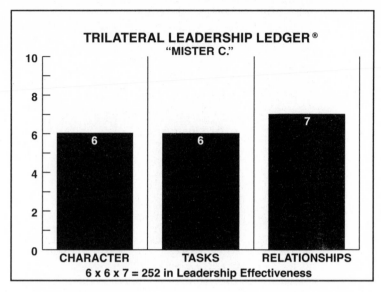

In this example it is obvious that people like Mister B. who have an area of significant weakness will hold themselves back until they grow in that area. It is not enough just to focus on strengths; weaknesses must also be addressed. Leaders do not have the luxury of being weak in any of these categories because of its catastrophic effect on their results. To be a leader, one must be strong in all three categories, period. It will take work, but that must be the goal. Otherwise, weaknesses will undo strengths. As famed Duke basketball coach Mike Krzyzewski once noted, "Never let a person's weakness get in the way of his strength."

Once a leader grasps this concept of personal growth and takes full responsibility for where he or she is on the Leadership Ledger, it is only a matter of time before the multiplying effect of improvement kicks in and external results are revealed.

A third example: Mister C. has been working diligently to become a leader for quite some time. He has followed the development process outlined in this book and has made conscious decisions to improve in all three areas on the Ledger. Last year, Mister C. rated himself a 6 for Character, a 6 for Tasks, and a 7 for Relationships. His total score was 6 times 6 times 7, for a total of 252.

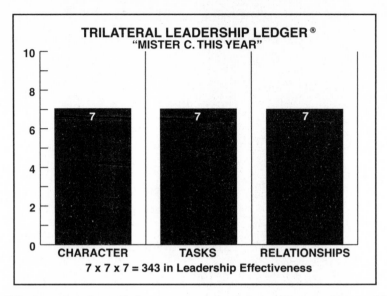

Working hard in all three categories, Mister C. raised himself by just one point in both Character and Tasks, but didn't feel he improved his ability any in the relationship area. His score now consists of 7 times 7 times 7, for a total leadership effectiveness of 343!

Mister C. raised his score 91 points, or 36 percent, and he improved only by a mere 1 point in two categories. What Mister C. is experiencing is the compounding effect of accumulated effort. Leadership has a compounding effect. It is the exponential return on effort obtained by a group of people aligned in common purpose that accomplish more than the sum of the whole.

This compounding effect is the very reason leaders influence other people. The Trilateral Leadership Ledger is a way that demonstrates and tracks a leader's improvement and scope of influence.

Sometimes we observe leaders who wield tremendous influence and have massive external results to show for their efforts. That is the power of compounding applied to human energy. All of the greatest leaders of history, who accomplished so much and left such an indelible mark on this planet and its people, utilized this compounding effect that only leadership can provide. Some did it through force, others through persuasion, still others through real altruism and concern for mankind; but for all of them, massive accomplishments required massive influence. The important thing to note is that this multiplier effect is available to anyone. It's just a decision to follow the leadership-development process and improve and grow in each of the categories.

Many people become curious about their own ranking using the Trilateral Leadership Ledger. As we stated before, a leader will most likely be fairly weak in all categories in the beginning. In fact, most people evaluating themselves for the first time will score much closer to 0 in each category than they will to 10. Additionally, many would-be leaders have zero overall influence because they are zeroed out in one of the categories. Think of the character issues of the leaders of Enron and Tyco and the high-profile corporate scandals of recent years. No matter how inspirational those leaders' leadership styles were, they have no long-term influence because of character problems. A deficiency of the same magnitude in either the task or relationship category will keep one from moving off of 0 as well.

Sometimes, however, a would-be leader's chief problem in using the Leadership Ledger is self-deception. To a certain degree, all human beings suffer from this ailment—we don't see ourselves exactly as the outside world sees us. In fact, one of the biggest impediments to growing and improving as a leader is the unwillingness or inability to see one's own "blind spots." We have encountered this repeatedly in our years of coaching business owners. An individual will think he or she is competent in a certain area when, in fact, he or she is extremely in need of improvement in exactly that category. One quip says that we tend to look at our own strengths while seeing everybody else's weaknesses. Reversing this tendency is a foundational requirement of leadership growth. We must confront reality about ourselves and, at the risk of sounding redundant, we must confront that reality as it really is! Without a true assessment how can one grow and improve and advance?

The Trilateral Leadership Ledger is a tool to begin this sometimes painful process. If honestly considered, it can disallow the blinding self-deception that prohibits so many people from moving on to bigger successes in life. If thoughtfully analyzed, the Trilateral Leadership Ledger can hone in on areas that require specific attention, identify major areas for improvement, and call attention to existing strengths. The good news is that a problem identified is a problem half solved. If there is an area that is hindering one from achieving his or her personal best, then a plan for improvement can be developed. In fact, that is the exact intent of this book.

Perhaps some specific estimates will be illustrative. We have found that an individual with a total score of 50 to 100 points is capable of leading smaller groups of people. Such a leader has the character to be followed, a solid work ethic, and an ability to get along with others. Moving upward to a total score of 200 to 300 puts one in rarer company. At this level one is capable of leading large groups of people (notice we didn't say *managing*) and has a near impeccable character score, a work ethic that inspires others, and an ability to create vision and mold a group into a solid team. A person with a score above 300 is a leader sought after by corporations and volunteer groups as a known influencer of people on a large scale. Very few will ever attain this level, but it is available to everyone willing to develop the art and science of leadership.

As leaders, and human ones at that, we will never arrive at perfection. The score of 1,000 is unattainable, but we should never cease in our pursuit of it, closing the gap between where we are and perfection on a regular basis. If we think we have arrived at "good enough," even for a moment, our progress will stop. Worse, it may even go backward. Too many stories can be told of great leaders rising to tremendous influence only to regress rapidly because of reversals in character, effort, or concern for others.

Personal Growth: Benjamin Franklin
"Arriving at Moral Perfection"

Benjamin Franklin was one of the United States' most distinguished and diverse founding fathers. He lived a long and prosperous life, lived a "rags to riches" story, spoke several languages, dined with ambassadors and philosophers, was published in many countries, enjoyed worldwide fame, and was one of the only signers of both the Declaration of Independence and the Constitution of the United States (and he also signed the Treaty of Paris ending the Revolutionary War). Franklin was the key architect of the alliance between the young United States of America and the world's second superpower, France, and in so doing he established the means of winning the war with England. He was the creator and writer of *Poor Richard's Almanac*, one of the most widely read annual publications in the New World. He invented bifocals, the enormously popular Franklin stove, and even a musical instrument for which Mozart composed a specific piece of music. His experiments in electricity thrilled the world and initiated the age of electrical discovery and application. He founded the American Philosophical Society, was instrumental in the birth of the University of Pennsylvania, established the first library in the colonies, and worked to organize the early fire departments in Philadelphia.

Franklin's life may best be considered in three distinct phases. First was his early life as a printer, writer, and businessman. In these years he learned to become a "gentleman" (even though he was not of "proper" birth, a major factor in his day), and amassed a fortune that would support him the rest of his life and outlive him by two centuries. The second phase was his time spent as a "natural philosopher" or scientist and inventor. It was during these years that his fame increased to international proportions, culminating in his membership and active participation in the English Philosophical Society. Finally, his later life was spent as a statesman, representing some of the English colonies on the North American coast and ultimately the fledgling United States of America.

How did he accomplish so much in just one lifetime? How did he rise so high to end up wielding such power and command so much respect around the world? The answers could fill volumes of books. The obvious, though, is that he was a genius. But even geniuses must follow the laws of success, and, besides, Benjamin Franklin's remarkable achievements were the result of his deliberate efforts. He was not lucky. He did not "back into" his accomplishments. He worked hard and tirelessly throughout his life.

There is a story Franklin himself tells in his autobiography about his troubles with relating to people as a young man. A confidant took him aside one day and was both bold and kind enough to share the truth with Franklin that people didn't like him. Although he was amazingly brilliant, nobody cared. They couldn't stand to be around him. He was too argumentative and opinionated. His informer even told him that people would see Franklin approaching on the street and cross the road so as to avoid any contact with him. Franklin was devastated. But his reaction to the cold, hard truth was perhaps one of the most important components in his meteoric success. As a young man, he decided to do something about it.

First, Franklin began tempering his statements to people so as not to offend. He worked hard to become less dogmatic in his choices of words and tones of voice. Then, a few years later, while sailing from England back to the colonies, he undertook "the bold and arduous Project of arriving at moral Perfection," commenting that "I was surprised to find myself so much fuller of faults than I had imagined." So Benjamin Franklin did what we've been discussing in this chapter: he deliberately set out upon a program of personal growth. He selected thirteen virtues he felt worthy of his attention and organized a demanding schedule of improvement and tracking. He would work on one virtue for four weeks at a time, recording his progress or lack thereof, then move on to the next virtue, repeating the cycle over and over throughout several years. Regarding his faults that had surprised him so much, he "had the satisfaction of seeing them diminish." As an old man he would say about his little project, "But on the whole, though I never arrived at the Perfection I had been so ambitious of obtaining, but fell far short of it, yet I was by the Endeavor made a better and a happier man than I otherwise should have been, if I had not attempted it; as those who aim at perfect writing by imitating the engraved copies, though they never reach the wished for excellence of those copies, their hand is mended by the endeavor, and is tolerable while it continues fair and legible."

Franklin's thirteen virtues were as follows. We have labeled them according to how they fit into the three categories represented on the Trilateral Leadership Ledger.

1. Temperance (Character)
2. Silence (Character, Relationships)
3. Order (Tasks)
4. Resolution (Tasks)
5. Frugality (Character, Tasks)
6. Industry (Tasks)
7. Sincerity (Character, Relationships)
8. Justice (Character, Relationships)
9. Moderation (Character)
10. Cleanliness (Character, Tasks)
11. Tranquility (Character)
12. Chastity (Character)
13. Humility (Character, Relationships)

Just as we have described the journey of personal growth for a leader involving self-assessment, willful change, and measurement of progress, Ben Franklin and his thirteen virtues followed the same principles.

With a reminder that improvement and growth is a self-guided mission, Franklin said, "We may give advice, but we cannot give conduct." Each leader must take it upon him- or herself to grow personally, just as Benjamin Franklin did. And if it was a worthy endeavor for a man of such genius, what may its worth be to the less endowed?

Summary

Personal growth is not an option for a leader. The Bible says that we will never be given more than we can handle. Therefore, if we want more, we must develop the capacity to handle more. The Trilateral Leadership Ledger is a tool both for instruction on the great principles of self-improvement and a tracking device for actual application. As leaders understand that their conduct is up to them and the amplification of their natural gifts is their responsibility, they will have set out upon the path of personal growth and increased effectiveness. As they take charge of improving personally, leaders can next begin embracing the idea of increasing their influence with others.

HOW A LEADER GROWS IN INFLUENCE

CHAPTER 5

The Five Levels of Influence

A true leader inspires others to lead themselves.

—ARI D. KAPLAN

Progressive Leadership is about the increasing ability of a leader to expand his or her *influence*. As a leader grows in ability, the leader's influence grows as well, but this is not an automatic process. If a leader is to maximize his potential and his influence, the process must be deliberate. Expanding the influence of a leader is accomplished by growing the leader himself.

The Five Levels of Influence are a convenient way to map the journey of a leader from beginning to crowning achievement. The leader grows in stature and ability to influence by ascending these steps. Each level presents more influence and takes greater advantage of the abilities of the leader by amplifying those abilities across a broader spectrum.

Levels of Leadership

The concept of various levels of leadership (and hence, influence) is found in several sources, but two stand out above the others.

The first is from renowned leadership expert John C. Maxwell in his book *Developing the Leader Within You*. Maxwell also suggests that there are Five Levels of Leadership, given here in ascending power of influence:

1. Position
2. Permission
3. Production
4. People Development
5. Personhood

Maxwell explains that Level 1, Position, is leadership based upon title alone. There is no credibility for this leader except for his official authority. Next is Permission, where a leader is allowed to lead because his followers allow it. Production is when followers pursue a leader because the leader gets results. People Development is when people like and respect the leader and experience an increased performance when dealing with that leader. Personhood is the rare condition when a leader has established a large following and achieved massive results based on his character and longevity. These levels help to make sense of the myriad of leadership ability encountered on a daily basis.

The second source for this idea of Levels of Leadership is Jim Collins, author of *Good to Great*. In that best-selling book, Collins presents the following Five Levels of Leadership, again in ascending order of effectiveness:

1. Capable Individual
2. Contributing Team Member

3. Competent Orchestrator
4. Effective Leader
5. Executive

Collins says a Capable Individual (Level 1) is someone who has obtained core competencies and basic abilities. A Contributing Team Member functions well as part of a group effort. A Competent Orchestrator is skilled at coordinating the efforts of Contributing Team Members. An Effective Leader is one with a broader vision and the ability to direct the Orchestrators toward big-picture objectives. And the highest elevation in Collins's hierarchy of leadership is the Executive, with whom full directional responsibility for the organization resides.

These experts on leadership have given us an enormous insight into clarifying a difficult subject. Mapping the path of a leader to greatness is no easy challenge, especially when the goal of that map is to provide a straightforward route for up-and-coming leaders. Maxwell and Collins have surveyed the wild country. It is the intention of this book to settle that territory into smaller, usable plots. Building upon their ideas and examining them at a pragmatic level will provide the developing leader with increased clarity on the leadership development process.

The Five Levels of Influence Explained

This concept of Levels of Influence will be explored within the framework of the following hierarchy:

1. Learning
2. Performing
3. Leading
4. Developing Leaders
5. Developing Developers of Leaders

As with Maxwell and Collins, these Five Levels are in ascending order, but they are slightly different from those of either author.

A previous diagram may be helpful here. Earlier we discussed the Foundational Qualities a leader must possess to gain entrance through the door and onto the playing field of leadership. Next were the Cycle of Achievement and personal growth. Now it is time to explore the playing field of leadership.

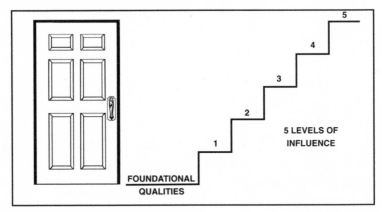

Note that the playing field is not level. It is more like a flight of ascending stairs. This is because as a leader progresses through the leadership-development process, his influence increases and the impact of his efforts have broader scope. Also, as the leader ascends the Levels of Influence, each of the previous levels stays with him. Just because a leader has advanced to the level of Performing doesn't mean he stops Learning. Likewise, a leader who advances to Developing Leaders cannot stop Leading in other areas, and so on.

So the Five Levels of Influence represent a progressive process where a leader picks up new abilities while accumulating and expanding his or her influence. A leader may be at various Levels of Influence in different areas of his or her life. Also, organizations themselves can exist at different levels on this progression. Finally, individuals within the organization each exist at their own Level of Influence. These realizations are helpful in pinpointing where individuals and organizations are, and for developing plans for growth and improvement.

Living the Five Levels of Influence: Queen Elizabeth I

Perhaps one of the best examples of a leader ascending through various levels of leadership is England's Queen Elizabeth I. Born in the tumultuous sixteenth century to the infamous King Henry VIII, Elizabeth proved her mettle at first by simply surviving. Her father had her mother executed, and Elizabeth was later framed in a complicated power struggle within the English royal court. This kept her under suspicion and confinement during the entire reign of her cousin, Edward VI. Then later, when her half-sister Mary I (later to be called Bloody Mary) gained control of the English throne, Elizabeth was in constant danger of being killed by order of the jealous and religiously opposite Queen. Elizabeth did not waste her time in confinement, however, but used it wisely by taking all the advantage she could of the education available to royalty.

Elizabeth's period of learning and survival finally gave birth to her chance to perform, as she attained the throne upon the death of Mary. As she became Queen, Elizabeth faced a country on the brink of civil war and, worse, she gained power in a time and place where women were not thought fit to rule. The privations of her sister before her didn't help matters, either. But Elizabeth's leadership ability was immediately apparent. According to author Alan Axelrod in *Profiles in Leadership*, "She quickly established a charismatic rapport with the crowds. . . . Elizabeth made it clear that she meant to return England . . . to greatness in trade and among the nations."

Elizabeth's next level of leadership was evidenced by her acute ability to surround herself with loyal talent. Axelrod states, "Celebrated for her strong will, Elizabeth nevertheless gathered about herself the best and brightest political and economic minds of England to serve as her advisers." This ever-increasing ring of power would eventually include such notables as Sir Francis Drake, John Hawkins, and Sir Walter Raleigh, who, as sea-faring adventurers, would be instrumental in defeating the mighty Spanish Armada (with some help from the weather). In the course of her reign Elizabeth had taken a chaotic and quarrelsome, economically tiny country and elevated it to the position of the most prosperous in Europe.

At her highest level of leadership influence, Elizabeth created a stable political climate and tradition that endured even after her death. It was during her reign of over four decades that English people developed a strong national pride and sense of "countryhood." This was to carry down through generations. As much as any leader, the life of Queen Elizabeth I demonstrates the results that are possible through the ascending levels of influence available to a leader.

Summary

Exploration of the Five Levels of Influence in the following chapters demonstrates that leadership is both an art (requiring thinking) and a science (requiring action). Arguments have raged for centuries as to whether leadership is an art, that is, based upon talent and largely "discerned" by the capable, or whether it is a science, meaning that it's simply skill based and can be "learned" by anyone. The upcoming pages contend that leadership is fairly considered to be *both* art and science.

For each of the Five Levels of Influence, there are presuppositions, or mind-sets, that are required for a leader to perform at that Level. This is the "art" portion of leadership. Yet each Level is not complete without actions, or the "science" side. The presuppositions will be discussed first because understanding the thinking behind actions always results in more effective actions.

The next several chapters assist developing leaders in discerning and understanding the thinking or "art" involved in leadership, while learning and applying the actions or "science" side.

CHAPTER 6

The First Level of Influence: Learning

That is one of the great secrets of becoming a great leader—never stop becoming.

—JEFF O'LEARY

The first of the Levels of Influence is becoming a student. Being hone-able and learning from others have already been stated as keys to leadership success, but here the concept is analyzed at greater depth.

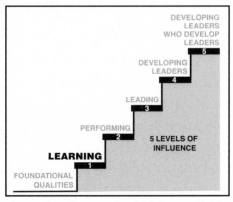

At this First Level of Influence, a leader is a little like a child running onto the field for her first soccer game. She is full of hunger and enthusiasm, but has a low level of skill and knows very little about the sport. It is not time to worry too much about winning. It is not time to be overly concerned with appearances or making impressions on the coach. It is time to *learn*.

Leaders must fall in love with learning. They must resist the temptation to be judgmental or critical or block out the fact that they have something to learn. Every great leader realizes that he still has more to discover. Author Andy Stanley observed, "Great leaders are great learners."

When taking on a new task or responsibility, a leader must be zealous to learn all there is to know. Leaders cannot expect to become experts in every area of operation, but they should never stop pursuing information and understanding. George Barna tells us, "You should always be involved in some type of intentional and focused study that is building up your leadership capacity." Learning is an attitude, and leaders must have a healthy dose of it. And a proper attitude regarding learning is critical right from the start of the leadership-development process. Stanley continues, "In the early years of your career, what you learn is far more important than what you earn. In most cases, what you learn early on will determine what you earn later on."

Presuppositions or the "Art" of Learning

When it comes to Level 1, would-be leaders must understand the foundational thought processes that open the doors to education. We call these presuppositions. Without a base of correct thinking, learning will be difficult and the proper learning activities will be resisted, missed, or at least not fully utilized, but when a leader understands the very *concept* of learning and the mentality upon which it is based, education can truly occur.

Learning Is a Top Priority

Initial and ongoing education is crucial for a leader. This education is not necessarily formal or "credentialed." Learning for a leader can occur in many ways. The key is that learning becomes a staple food in the mental diet of the leader. At Level 1, leaders must realize that they are only as good as what they learn and apply.

Leaders Can Learn from Anyone

Leaders must be aware that opportunities for learning are all around them. Education, information, insight, and wisdom can come from any source. Nobody is "below" the leader. Something can be learned from anyone. As Dale Carnegie wrote, "Everyone is your superior in some way."

Leaders Can Learn Best from Those Who Have Results

Although it is true that something can be learned from anybody, it is equally true that *the best education comes from those who have results in life*,

> *The best education comes from those who have results in life.*

in particular, those who have success in the exact area of concern where the leader operates. Doesn't it make sense to learn about becoming a physician from a successful doctor? Wouldn't the information about starting a business be most valuable from a successful entrepreneur? As the saying goes, "Success begins with information from the correct source."

Actions or the "Science" of Learning

Standing firmly on the aforementioned presuppositions, the student can then focus on the actions or science side of learning. These can be considered the *skills* of learning, or what a leader learns *about*.

Leaders Learn About People

Leaders know that people are what leadership is all about, and they understand that it is only through people that leaders have influence. It is *with*, *through*, and *for* people that leadership exists.

Perhaps you've heard the cliché that "an organization's most important resource is its people." The statement should actually be refined to say, "An organization's best resource is the *right* people," for the right people are the heart of progress while the wrong people are just the opposite (and everybody knows that the opposite of "pro-gress" is "con-gress"). Therefore, leaders must become experts at dealing with people, and determining who the *right* people are to hire, recruit, train, and develop. This is true in both a general and a specific sense.

> It is *with*, *through*, and *for people that leadership exists.*

First of all, leaders must be well disciplined in the art of human relations, and this cannot be only at a superficial, surface level. There is nothing worse than a would-be leader pumped full of people skills but operating from a devious heart. This is precisely why character is such a critical element. It is so critical, in fact, that one shouldn't even be allowed onto the leadership playing field without it. So it is assumed, if a leader has gotten this far and is beginning the ascent of the Five Levels of Influence, that character is a given. The reason is that people don't care how much a leader knows until they know *how much he cares.* If the leader has character and his heart is right, people will trust and follow him. Then and only then do people *skills* come into play, and these skills are very important. A leader should be learning in this critical area all the time.

Second, a leader must learn about his people *specifically*. This is an extension of people wanting to know that the leader cares. Great leaders take an active, sincere interest in other people. In *How to Win Friends and Influence People*, Dale Carnegie tells us that we should picture everyone we meet as wearing an invisible sign around his neck that says, "Make me feel important." Everyone wants to be acknowledged and accepted. *Great leaders understand this and make it a point to treat their people as special, learning as much as they can about them.* This includes remembering names and details of the person's life. One of the most effective ways for leaders to learn about each of their people is to find something in common with them. Picture a boat circling an island, looking for a port at which to dock. A connection is made when the boat makes landfall and snuggles safely into the harbor. Leaders must connect with their people in a similar fashion, taking the time to circle and discover a point of commonality where contact can be made and a relationship can be initiated.

Learning how to deal with people in a general sense, and learning *about* them in a specific and caring way, is an ongoing process for any leader.

Leaders Learn About Basics

Everything a leader knows at the top she learns at the bottom. This is the part of the leadership-development process where the leader gains an intricate knowledge of the fundamentals in her field. Learning the basics is not optional. Under no circumstances can a successful leader skip this step. As the leader begins to perform and make mistakes, she falls forward, gets up, and tries again. It is in this "productive loop" where the leader becomes strong and capable.

John Wooden, legendary coach of the UCLA basketball team that won ten championships and had eight straight undefeated seasons, tells a story in his book *Wooden, A Lifetime of Observations On and Off the Court.* For years, Coach Wooden would begin each season with a new team by giving them detailed instructions on the proper way to wear tube socks. This involved turning the socks inside out and removing the balled-up clumps of cloth often left there by the manufacturing process. Apparently these pieces of cloth could cause blisters, which would obviously have an enormously negative impact on a player's performance. Imagine taking the time for such a small detail! But Wooden was reinforcing timeless fundamentals with which every player must begin, and reinforcing the importance of mastering basics.

Leaders Learn About Goals and Objectives

Leaders must learn all they can about the goals and objectives that are required or expected of their organization. An organization cannot hit a target that doesn't exist, and it is a leader's job to learn all there is to learn about the group's requirements. This is doubly important because it also falls to the leader to articulate a vision to the organization of achieving the goals that are before them.

Leaders Learn About Processes

Understanding the processes involved in their areas is a necessity for leaders. It will be the responsibility of the leader to evaluate these processes and perhaps make adjustments and improvements, but this will be premature if the leader has not worked to master the processes. Learning all there is to know about the processes will also give the leader credibility when dealing with subordinates who may be closer to and more involved with the daily details. Then, leaders can work with the people in the organization either to make improvements in the processes or to ensure that the existing processes are executed properly.

Leaders Learn About Measurements of Performance

Leaders must thoroughly learn the metrics used to determine performance levels in their organization. This is true in a large, overall sense, and also at the detail level for each of the people in the leader's sphere of influence. Leaders cannot operate solely on "feel." There must be concrete measurements of performance that provide the leader with ongoing feedback. Billionaire founder of

Microsoft Corporation, Bill Gates, calls it "Business at the Speed of Thought." In his book of the same title, Gates makes the point that performance data are crucial to the agility and survival of an organization. If data are faster and more relevant, better choices can be made by the leaders.

Leaders Learn About Rewards

No leader can lead without a solid understanding of the rewards of performance in his field. This is true for himself personally, and for the people in his organization. This is because motivation is critical to proper casting of vision and maximizing performance. A leader who neglects to learn all there is to learn in this critical category leaves a valuable weapon in the holster.

Leaders Learn about Histories

"Those who cannot remember the past are condemned to repeat it," said philosopher George Santayana. Leaders must take an active interest in the history of their organization. There are valuable lessons to be learned that can save time and energy. To neglect these clues from the past is shortsighted and will only come to haunt the leader. Not knowing the lessons of the past also compromises the leader's credibility with his people, who may have actually lived through some of the events.

A big part of learning the history of an organization is learning about its successes. Who has made it big? How did they do it? Why did they experience success? Are they available for firsthand instruction? What processes seemed to work the best? What innovations were implemented? What could have been done to bring an even bigger impact? What were the pitfalls that were avoided? Asking these types of questions and studying up on the successes of the past are an allowable shortcut every leader should pursue.

It has been said that we learn more from our failures than we ever do from our successes. This is true at the organizational level as well. Leaders should continually be doing "crash test analyses" to discover what didn't work and why. Learning what doesn't work brings the leader one step closer to what does work. Failure is not failure if something is learned from it. *Failure that teaches a lesson is simply tuition toward a future success.* As leaders endeavor to lead, they will make mistakes and experience failures. Astute leaders know to extract every ounce of lesson from each mistake, understanding that the lesson continues until the lesson is learned. Great leaders are not those who never make mistakes. Great leaders are those who learn quickly and most effectively from their mistakes.

Leaders Learn About Environment

In *Authentic Leadership* Bill George writes, "The leader's job is to provide an empowering environment." Leaders must learn about the environments in their organizations and use that knowledge to enhance and maximize it. As with so many of the responsibilities of a leader, learning about and optimizing the organization's environment is never complete. People need an empowering, exciting, positive, encouraging environment where mistakes are accepted as long as they are learned from, where success is rewarded, and where processes make sense and get results. Under such conditions, people in an organization can thrive. The archway over all of this is the leader's own attitude and outlook. This, more than anything else, sets the tone for the organization and creates the right environment. Smart leaders never stop learning about their organization's environment and ways to enhance it.

Leaders Learn About Obstacles and Oppositions

Roadblocks are scattered all along the highway of success. Leaders are wise to be diligent and knowledgeable about these pitfalls. Learning about obstructions in the path to achievement and properly defining them is a necessary part of continual learning.

Many leaders tend to continue hammering away at the same old challenges without ever stopping to see if they are having an effect. Einstein wrote, "Insanity: doing the same thing over and over again and expecting different results." Leaders must seek to understand what may be holding them back and properly quantify the situation. Only then can plans be implemented for the removal of the obstacle. Remember, properly defining a problem is the biggest part of solving it. Learning about obstacles and challenges to an organization also gives the leader information to share with mentors in seeking ways to resolve them.

Along with obstacles comes opposition. It seems that no matter what a leader's undertaking, there will always be someone opposed to it. Learning all that can be done to neutralize those in opposition to a leader's goals can be crucial to the organization's success. Often, though, simply ignoring those in opposition is the best course of action. No leader ever accomplishes anything without someone saying it can't be done. You've heard the old saying, "Leaders are busy doing the things critics say can't be done." Usually, the best antidote for criticism is success. Learning that principle may be one of a leader's most important lessons.

When he or she understands these *areas* of learning, or what a leader learns about, a leader should then take full advantage of all *methods* of learning available, or the sources from which a leader learns.

Leaders Learn from Books

Harry Truman said, "Not all readers are leaders, but all leaders must be readers." It is a fact that most of the greatest leaders throughout history have been avid readers. As a young boy, Napoleon read books constantly. President Teddy Roosevelt was known to read at least a book a day, and sometimes two,

> *"Not all readers are leaders, but all leaders must be readers."*

even while president! Thomas Jefferson bought books compulsively throughout his life and read them with even more vigor than he collected them. Singer and songwriter Jimmy Buffett said of his mother, "She taught me that reading is the key to everything."

Books represent the accumulated knowledge and wisdom of the ages, available for pennies on the dollar. Books preserve the greatest thoughts, the greatest ideas, and the greatest insights of human experience. Roy L. Smith said, "A good book contains more wealth than a good bank." Reading a book puts one in touch with an author the reader may never have a chance to meet in person, either because of distance or time. And reading is one of the best, most time-tested avenues to leadership experience. If other people's experience is the best teacher, books are the best transmitter of that experience. True leaders know this and make reading a consistent part of their plan for success. Jim Rohm observes, "If you read a book a week, in a year you'll have read 52 books. In ten years 520 books. You'll be in the top 1% of your field. You'll be more motivated, better educated; you'll become the leader in your field."

> *"Reading is a means of thinking with another person's mind: It forces you to stretch your own."*

William J. O'Neil, founder of *Investor's Business Daily*, tells us, "People who hope to successfully influence what goes on around them will develop the habit of reading great books." Ralph Waldo Emerson wrote, "Many times the reading of a book has made the future of a man."

Perhaps one of the greatest reading stories of all time is billionaire entertainer Oprah Winfrey, whose television program reaches over 20 million viewers a day in over 130 countries. Glamorous, smart, and successful, she didn't start out that way. Born in Mississippi to a poor, unwed mother, Oprah was at first handed off to an uneducated grandmother, then at age six to her father and step-mother. It was there that she received her first access to a library and the encouragement to read. Her father even required her to write him book reports on what she read, and limited her television time to a maximum of one hour a day. When asked about her success, Oprah once said, "It all started because I was a great reader." Of her lifelong love of reading and her passion to encourage others to do the same through her now-famous book club, she said, "I want to help people create the highest vision for themselves. It's one thing to win an Emmy. It's another thing to influence somebody who hasn't picked up a book since they were forced to in high school and for them to start thinking differently about their own life as a result of that."

Sometimes when we tout the benefits of reading, people assume we mean reading for entertainment. "Oh good!" they say, "I already read several novels a month." Certainly there is an entertainment value to reading. But when we speak of reading good books, we are not referring to the latest dime-store thriller that keeps one turning pages or to the type of books that can be "read in one sitting." As evangelist and writer A. W. Tozer said, "The best book is the one that sets us off on a train of thought that carries us far away from and far beyond the book itself." Our reading should be guided by our need and desire to grow as leaders, fashioning us into better people. Noted eighteenth-century scholar Dr. Samuel Johnson once sat in discussion with the King of England. "I suppose, Dr. Johnson, that you read a great deal," said the King. "Yes, Sire," replied Johnson, "but I *think* a great deal more." Our reading should not just be for enjoyment, but should foster growth in our minds and persons. Reading should lead to better thoughts, which in turn lead to better actions, which then lead to better habits, which then produce better results, which then produce a better future.

From leaders like George Washington, Thomas Jefferson,

Abraham Lincoln, Theodore Roosevelt, and Harry Truman, to writers like Ralph Waldo Emerson, Henry David Thoreau, and Ernest Hemingway, to entertainers like Oprah Winfrey, Jimmy Buffett, and Woody Allen, to historical figures like Socrates, Diderot, Gustave Flaubert, and Francis Bacon, leaders are encouraged over and over to make reading a regular part of their diet. As perhaps only Mark Twain could say, "The man who does not read good books has no advantage over the man who can't read them."

Leaders Learn from Audio Recordings

It is almost a universal rule that ambitious people are busy. The type of people who would invest the time to read a book on leadership certainly fit that description. So what is one of the most effective methods of learning on a continual basis in the midst of such a busy life? The answer is audio recordings.

In nearly every field of endeavor, audio recordings are available on cassette, on compact disc, or in other mediums. They are convenient sources of learning and inspiration because they can be played almost anywhere a leader goes. Many of today's most successful leaders make it a habit to listen to audio recordings in their car whenever possible. It has been said that any subject studied for thirty minutes a day for five years makes one an expert on that subject. If that is true, audio recordings are one of education's greatest tools!

Audio recordings also have the added benefit of teaching through what the listener hears. This involves a different set of brain functions than does reading. The two together make a potent combination. Some people learn more by what they see, while others learn more from what they hear. A steady diet of book reading and listening to audio recordings blends these two learning methods and maximizes the leader's education.

Finally, leaders should search to find audio recordings produced by top performers in their field. By this method, leaders can take advantage of the principle of learning from the experience of others, and actually be learning from many mentors at once. In some cases, this will be the only exposure leaders have to mentors until they succeed at a higher level.

Great leaders know that "listening time" is not for entertainment, but for education. And true leaders take every advantage they can get, accomplishing more than one thing at a time. There is a tremendous economy of time to be gained when listening to an audio recording while driving a car, taking a shower, or performing mindless chores. Leaders understand the power of passive education through listening and the advantages to be gained by multitasking as a way to optimize their educational opportunities.

Leaders Learn from Videos

Videos in large part combine the benefits of reading and listening to audio recordings, in that they provide something for both the visual and the audio learner. Videos can also be an extremely clear form of communication where graphs, charts, photographs, and other forms of graphics are beneficial. Famous sales trainer and author Zig Ziglar said that over two-thirds of communication is "non-verbal." Videos help the learner capture the visual components of communication along with the audio ones, thereby enhancing comprehension.

Leaders pursue every avenue of learning available to them in their quest for increased leadership effectiveness, and that often includes a steady intake of instructional and informational videos.

Leaders Learn from Association with Other Successful Leaders

"Birds of a feather flock together," goes the old saying. "Tell me who you hang around and I'll tell you all about you," says another. "We are a product of the books we read, the things we listen to, and the people we associate with," says yet another. These sayings all ring with the same truth: that we become a lot like the people with whom we choose to associate. For this reason, leaders must seek out and associate with other leaders.

This can and should be done interpersonally, as well as through seminars and symposiums in the areas of leadership and in the leader's specific field. There is something magical about gathering with other like-minded leaders who are in pursuit of common goals. Attending seminars and conferences reinforces the leader's convictions and beliefs in his endeavor and builds relationships with other leaders that can last a lifetime and be mutually beneficial. Author James Autry quotes a business client as saying, "Our business is built on relationships. I feel [those on our team] have to associate with other company people, and they have to be members of something. Because without that association, that sense of membership in something, or to put that a better way, without a sense of belonging and participation in a group effort, the [person] loses focus on what we're trying to accomplish together."

Robert Kiyosaki said, "Your income will be the average of the five people you hang around the most." But the most poignant story about the power of association comes from Mark Victor Hansen, co-author of the wildly popular *Chicken Soup for the Soul* book series. Earlier in his career he had the opportunity to meet with success coach and author Tony Robbins. Robbins inquired as to the income level of the people Hansen associated with on a regular basis to discuss careers and share ideas. Hansen replied that the range was $5 million to $6 million per year. Robbins replied that everyone in his own group of affiliation earned around $100 million per year, and that explained their obvious difference in incomes!

While most of us don't start out having access to the fabulously successful, we can make every effort to read great books and attend conferences and seminars featuring those who have succeeded in our chosen field. It only makes sense that by associating with success we will begin to understand the thinking behind that success more clearly. Then, if it should come to pass that we get the opportunity to spend time with those of a much higher level of success than ourselves, we must treat the time with respect and value it for the learning opportunity it is!

Leaders Learn from Coaches and Mentors

We have already discussed the many reasons why seeking counsel is critical in the growth and development of a leader. Credible coaches and mentors have what can be called "fruit on the tree," meaning that they have accomplished significantly in the areas in which a leader operates, or they have proven themselves adept at developing those in the leader's field. Andy Stanley writes in *The Next Generation Leader*, "You will never maximize your potential in any area without coaching. It is impossible. You may be good. You may even be better than everyone else. But without outside input you will never be as good as you can be. We all do better when someone else is watching and evaluating."

There is a fine line of difference between the terms "coach" and "mentor" as we will be using them in this book. A coach is someone who encourages, guides, and develops the *performance* of another. A mentor is someone who helps mold and develop the very makeup and character of another. Leaders should seek and find credible coaches and mentors and utilize them on a regular basis as the cornerstone of their learning process.

Leaders Learn from Action

The methods of learning we've been discussing could be classified as theoretical in nature, but theory carries the learning process only so far. An old proverb says, "Do not let all your learning lead to knowledge; let it lead to action." Theory is not an education in itself; it is the warm-up for actual experience.

An apprentice once asked his master how he obtained such great wisdom. "Wisdom comes from good judgment," answered the master. "But how does one obtain good judgment?" asked the apprentice. "By experiencing enough bad judgment," answered the master.

It is not enough just to "experience" experiences. Wisdom is not the by-product of the passage of time. Evaluated experience is where true education occurs. Leaders should test everything they learn against the question, How can I apply this to what I'm doing? as well as, How can I learn from what just occurred? According to Warren Bennis, "Leaders learn by leading, and they learn best by leading in the face of obstacles." Theory actively *applied to experience* is a leader's best schoolmaster.

> Do not let all your
> learning lead to
> knowledge; let it lead
> to action.

Leaders Learn by Controlling the Flow

Education does not merely consider what should be included but also focuses on what should be left out. This is called "controlling the flow." A leader closely controls the quality of what is allowed into his brain. On a daily basis there is an inundation of information and viewpoints, opinions, commentaries, gossips, slanders, libels, misinformation, propaganda, and just plain "junk food for the brain." It becomes necessary to filter out as much of what is not fruitful for growth as possible. This may involve the breaking of some bad habits, which could include too much television, news, newspapers, and talk radio. This is necessary for many reasons.

> Focus involves blocking
> out distractions as
> much as it involves
> zeroing in on the goal
> at hand.

First, the modern media in all its forms simply takes too much time. Diogenes, the third-century Greek writer, said, "Time is the most valuable thing a man can spend." Leaders guard their time very jealously and know that each hour is precious. Time wasted bathing in useless media is time taken from more important endeavors, and it is certainly time spent away from learning anything valuable. A hallmark of great leaders is their intensity of focus. Focus involves blocking out distractions as much as it involves zeroing in on the goal at hand. The time regained by turning off the television or radio is time that can be better utilized listening to audio recordings, reading good books, or thinking and planning.

Second, the predominant message conveyed through the bulk of the national media is one of "celebrating mediocrity." Attitudes and norms that are anything but normal are paraded through the various media of our day and have a debilitating effect on our attitudes. We begin to call the abnormal normal and the normal abnormal. A leader's strongest weapon is his standard of character and absolute values. To allow the erosion of these for the purpose of "entertainment" or "staying informed" is irresponsible. Remember, leaders have the future of others in their hands. If their direction is to be clear, their heads must be also.

The Bible says, "Whatever is true, whatever is honorable, whatever is right, whatever is pure, whatever is lovely, whatever is of good repute, if there is any excellence and if anything worthy of praise, let your mind dwell on these things" (Philippians 4:8). Controlling the Flow is controlling the thoughts on which your mind dwells.

Active Learning: Theodore Roosevelt "A Campaign of Self-Transformation"

He was born into wealth in the eastern United States in the "Silk Stocking" district. But he was feeble (once referred to as a "pitiful specimen"), suffered incessantly from asthma, had tiny little legs, and was routinely picked on by bullies. When he was still a preadolescent boy his father said to him, "You have the mind but you have not the body, and without the help of the body the mind cannot go as far as it should. You must *make* your body. It is hard drudgery to make one's body, but I know you will do it."

Then one day he happened across a poem titled "The Flight of the Duchess" by Robert Browning, which described a young duke as:

> The prettiest little ape
> That ever affronted human shape.
> All that the old Dukes had been without knowing it
> This Duke would feign know he was, without being it.

As he told an interviewer toward the end of his life, that poem and the image of himself contained in its words propelled him into action.

Theodore Roosevelt's father assembled a "home gym" for his timid, delicate son, and the son went to work with vigor. Already interested in learning and having recently discovered that much of his clumsiness was due to his need for eyeglasses, the young scion also turned up the intensity of his self-education to a feverish pace that would continue throughout his life.

It wasn't long before young "Teddy" was gaining strength and confidence in himself. His personal diary shows a noted decline in sicknesses following that period, and in the month of August of 1871 he appears to have managed an entire month of good health, his longest such period in years. He began climbing mountains and swimming in icy rapids, and discovered his keen interest in natural science. He read tirelessly, causing one friend of the family to call him "the most studious little brute I ever knew in my life." But as an incident would show him, young Theodore Roosevelt had a long way to go. In his own words:

> Having an attack of asthma, I was sent off by myself to Moosehead Lake. On the stage-coach ride thither, I encoun-

tered a couple of other boys who were about my own age, but very much more competent and also much mischievous. They found that I was a foreordained and predestined victim, and industriously proceeded to make life miserable for me. The worst feature was that when I finally tried to fight them I discovered that either one singly could not only handle me with easy contempt, but handle me so as not to hurt me much and yet prevent my doing any damage whatever in return.

According to Pulitzer Prize-winning biographer Edmund Morris, "The humiliation forced [Roosevelt] to realize that his two years of body-building had achieved only token results. No matter how remarkable his progress might seem to himself, by the harsh standards of the world he was still a weakling. There and then he decided to join what he would later call 'the fellowship of the doers.' If he had exercised hard before, he must do so twice as hard now."

Roosevelt began boxing and hunting and all manners of "strenuous" activity. When he lost time in his studies to sickness, he would implore his tutor to double up on lessons so he wouldn't fall behind. His family, having significant means, traveled the world, and through those broadening journeys young Roosevelt gained knowledge eagerly as he boated down the Nile or climbed the great pyramids.

Eventually, Roosevelt's efforts paid off. He began showing signs of the robust chest muscles that would later be world famous, and he had formed the habits of reading, learning, and inquiring that would carry him throughout his amazing adult accomplishments.

Then, at age twenty-two, during a routine physical examination as he was about to graduate from college, Roosevelt was informed that he had a weak heart. Any strenuous activity could be a great health risk, and Theodore Roosevelt was strongly cautioned to live a sedentary life. To do otherwise, he was told, was to flirt with death. Roosevelt responded immediately and abruptly, saying, "Doctor, I am going to do all the things you tell me not to do. If I've got to live the sort of life you have described, I don't care how short it is."

Roosevelt was true to his pronouncements. He worked harder and longer and was soon surpassing others in physical stamina and athletic ability. One of his boxing partners complimented his work ethic and sheer determination by calling him a "manufactured" rather than a "natural" athlete. Roosevelt himself said, "Having been a rather sickly and awkward boy, I was as a young man at first both nervous and distrustful of my own prowess. I had to train myself painfully and laboriously not merely as regards my body but as regards my soul and spirit." James M. Strock wrote in *Theodore Roosevelt on Leadership*, "[He] undertook increasingly daring feats. He sought more than bodily exercise, expressing admiration for 'the sports which develop such qualities as courage, resolution, and endurance.'" In his autobiography, Roosevelt wrote:

> There are two kinds of success, or rather two kinds of ability displayed in the achievement of success. There is, first, the success . . . which comes to the man who has in him the natural power to do what no one else can do, and what no amount of training, no perseverance or will power, will enable any ordinary man to do. This is the most striking kind of success, and it can be attained only by the man who has in him the quality which separates him in kind no less than in degree from his fellows. But much the commoner type of success in every walk of life and in every species of efforts is that which comes to the man who differs from his fellows not by the kind of quality which he possesses but by the degree of development which he has given that quality. This kind of success is open to a large number of persons, if only they seriously determine to achieve it. It is the kind of success which is open to the average man . . . who has no remarkable mental or physical attributes, but who gets just as much as possible in the way of work out of the aptitudes that he does possess. It is only this kind of success that is open to most

of us. Yet some of the greatest successes in history have been those of this second class.

Upon the theme of this "second class of success," Roosevelt's life became a campaign of self-transformation. He would later say, "I never won anything without hard labor and the exercise of my best judgment and careful planning and working long in advance." In *The Rise of Theodore Roosevelt*, Edmund Morris said, "Even [his] 'free' periods were packed with mental, physical, or social activity. 'He was forever at it,' said one classmate. Another marveled: 'Never have I seen or read of a man with such an amazing array of interests.' Tumbling into bed at midnight or in the small hours, Theodore could luxuriate in healthy tiredness, satisfied that he had wasted not one minute of his waking hours."

Elting Morison wrote, "There is apparent throughout his life a surprising determination. The energies and talents he possessed were not placed at birth in some natural harmony; they were through the passing years organized and directed by a sustained and splendid act of will." According to James M. Strock, "Learning was, literally, a vital part of Roosevelt's leadership—a living force. His preparation for leadership through self-mastery began with books at his side. His years of leadership were constantly informed and enlarged by reading and writing, conversation, correspondence, and an extraordinarily broad . . . quest for experience. Roosevelt's thirst for learning was never quenched. As an executive [Roosevelt] frequently developed special relationships with . . . experts, going beyond the transmission of information and knowledge."

Roosevelt's program of self-mastery and determined learning spawned a fruitful life that is almost intimidating to review. He traveled extensively from the pyramids of Egypt to the Amazon jungle to the castles of Europe to safaris in Africa and cattle drives in the American West. He served in the New York National

Guard. He later formed his own regiment during the Spanish-American War and gained national fame as the fearless commander who led these "Rough Riders" up San Juan Hill to victory in Cuba. He purchased and ran a cattle ranch in Badlands Dakota Territory when the West was truly still "wild."

During one winter, bandits stole his rowboat from the river running through his ranch property. In the heart of a blizzard he followed them many miles upstream and captured them at gunpoint, tied them up, and transported them back to town. When not on these adventures, Roosevelt founded the National Collegiate Athletic Association and became president of the American Historical Association. He wrote thirty-eight books. And along the way, he was a dedicated and active husband and father.

He held many different public offices: president of the New York City Police Commission; mayor of New York City; assistant secretary of the navy; governor of New York; vice-president of the United States, and then in his early forties became (and remains) the youngest-ever president of the United States. His efforts as president resulted in the setting aside of 230 million acres of land as protected national reserves and parks, including Yellowstone, the Grand Canyon, and Yosemite. He was instrumental in initiating the revolution that led to the creation of the country of Panama and the resultant construction of the Panama Canal. His administration created the Commerce Department, the Department of Labor, the U.S. Forest Service, and significantly strengthened the U.S. Navy. He initiated the creation of the Food and Drug Act and the Federal Employers' Liability Act, all while reducing the national debt by $90 million. He mediated the Portsmouth Treaty ending the Russo-Japanese War. He was even the first American to win the Nobel Prize and was posthumously awarded the Medal of Honor, making him the only American ever to win both awards.

Roosevelt once shook 8,150 hands in one day, landing him a

place in the *Guinness Book of World Records*. Roosevelt was also one of the first Americans to fly in an airplane and one of the first to go underwater in a submarine, and remains the only national figure to be shot in the chest at point-blank range and subsequently give a ninety-minute speech before seeking medical attention. (The bullet remained in his massive chest muscles until his death over six years later.)

After reading this extremely impressive and diverse list of accomplishments, it is important to remember that Roosevelt himself ascribed all his achievements to the "second class" of success, the kind worked for and sought out deliberately. As Hermann Hagedorn concluded, "The story of Theodore Roosevelt is the story of a small boy who read about great men and decided that he wanted to be like them . . . and succeeded." Strock said, "Roosevelt viewed himself as a self-made man, in the sense that he 'made' his body, simultaneously fortifying his mind and spirit."

Theodore Roosevelt stands as perhaps the best example available of the principle of the First Level of Influence. He took an honest assessment of where he was personally in all respects—intellectually, spiritually, physically, and emotionally—and realized that *he didn't know what he didn't know*. Then he set about doing something about it. He sought education in all its forms (*We are only as good as what we learn*), including reading, traveling, learning from many different people, mentoring with experts, asking and listening, and, most of all, through his enormous capacity for action, *applying* all he learned to his daily life. He saw learning as one of life's highest joys and privileges, and he engaged in it with voracity, *continuing to learn and grow and change* throughout his energetic life. Stuck at the First Level of Influence throughout his youth, he would eventually shatter its confines and race up the ascending stairs of influence, saying, "Life brings sorrows and joys alike. It is what a man does with them—not what they do to him—that is the true test of his mettle."

Summary

Leaders do not graduate from Level 1 and move up the Levels of Influence unless they have mastered the fundamentals of learning. Learning must become a consistent way of life if a leader is to survive. It is at this First Level of Influence that a leader develops and continues to develop the skills that will carry him or her throughout the challenges ahead. Through the learning process, the leader's competency should become obvious to all. It is when this begins happening that the leader advances to the Second Level of Influence.

CHAPTER 7

The Second Level of Influence: Performing

When your work speaks for itself, don't interrupt.

—HENRY J. KAISER

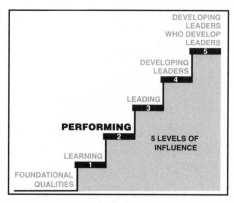

The second of the Five Levels of Influence is to become a Performer. If a leader never progressed beyond Level 1, she would not really accomplish much. That is because, more than any other level, the First Level is largely prepara-tory for the levels to come. It is at the Second Level where accomplishment begins. In this chapter, the terms Level 2 Leader and Performance will be used interchangeably.

At the Second Level of Influence the child soccer player from the last chapter is now focusing on fundamental performance. She is continuing to learn, of course, but her top priority is scoring goals, blocking shots, and becoming a key player on her team.

Presuppositions or the "Art" of Performing

Becoming a Performer requires a certain mind-set. It starts with the correct presuppositions or mentalities. Without the right frame of mind, without the proper assumptions, the thoughts a person has will significantly limit his or her performance. Proper thinking is the foundation of proper actions, and proper actions are what give birth to performance. So to become a Performer, which is a major step on the road to becoming a leader, one must internalize and operate according to several presuppositions.

Performers Understand that Results Come through Personal Effort

At the Second Level of Influence, the leader's accomplishments are mostly her own. Her influence extends only as far as her own ability to perform, and no further. But the Second Level is critical, and can have significant impact, as we will see. It is also a prerequisite to any Levels of Leadership that follow.

Performers Understand that Champions Don't Start Out that Way

For those new to the topic of success or leadership, it seems common to assume that champions have always been successful. Nothing could be a bigger myth. Champions become that way only through the commitment that follows a decision to be great. That commitment then gets applied to learning, growing, changing, performing, adjusting, and improving. Apply this formula, over time, with enthusiasm, and *that's* where champions originate. They do not start out that way.

Golf sensation Tiger Woods is a dominant player. He has won almost every golf title imaginable. To many, his appearance on the international golf scene seemed to come abruptly and "out of nowhere." In fact, his journey to the top was long, arduous, and actually *planned.* At age five, on a national television show Woods was shown practicing daily in order to "beat Jack Nicklaus" someday. That was quite a goal for anyone, much less a five-year-old! But Tiger Woods would live to achieve that goal, and hundreds of others.

> *"Actually, I'm an overnight success. But it took twenty years!"*

Over and over again in the stories of achievers we see that champions don't start out that way. As Monty Hall said, "Actually, I'm an overnight success. But it took twenty years!"

Performers Know There Will Be Many Opportunities to Feel Second Best

Sometimes people struggle to become Performers and find themselves smack up against a poor self-image. Additionally, there seems to be no shortage of situations that expose us to these feelings of inadequacy. We all have them. But Performers know that they must succeed despite these feelings, not in the absence of them. It is a decision. Sometimes we will not feel worthy of a certain accomplishment, so we must make ourselves worthy. We may not feel that we can measure up to our goals, and that is precisely the reason for deliberate personal growth. Because our potential outreaches our current reality, it is natural to feel a tinge of inadequacy. Personal growth closes that gap. To reach our potential, growth isn't optional. It is required. Performers take their feelings of inadequacy and turn them around, preferring to see them as measurements of their full potential.

Performers Understand that Nothing Worthwhile Comes Easy

President Theodore Roosevelt said, "There has not yet been a person in our history who led a life of ease whose name is worth remembering."

Success will not come easy, and if it does, it's not really success. Those who win the lottery often lose their winnings within a few years and end up further behind financially than before they bought the ticket. This is because they learned nothing and had no personal growth that *earned* the wealth, and without the lessons that earning wealth brings, wealth cannot be held.

> *Success is always located on the other side of inconvenience*

Success exacts a price, but it also delivers a prize. There will always be an exchange of effort for reward. Performers know that nothing good comes easy, nor do they expect things to happen overnight. They know that success is always located on the other side of inconvenience. Becoming a Performer requires a maturity that works for something not yet seen, has faith in an outcome only imagined, and persists when others quit.

Effort fully releases its reward only after a person refuses to quit. Persistence is the key. Robert Strauss said of success, "It's a little like wrestling a gorilla. You don't quit when you're tired—you quit when the gorilla is tired."

Performers Don't Expect Fair Treatment

Watch any group of children playing and it will be only a matter of time before one of them yells, "That's not fair." Even at a young age we seem to have a sense of fair play, a sense of justice. Performers know that in life there will be no shortage of situations that are "not fair." There will be no shortage of people who do us wrong, who cheat, lie, and steal, and who are just plain hurtful to others. Performers take this into account and strive for excellence anyway, focusing upon only what they can control.

On the wall of Mother Teresa's children's home in Calcutta was found the following inscription:

ANYWAY

People are unreasonable, illogical and self-centered.
LOVE THEM ANYWAY.
If you do good, people will accuse you of selfishness.
DO GOOD ANYWAY.
If you are successful you will win false friends and true enemies.
SUCCEED ANYWAY.
The good you do will be forgotten tomorrow.
DO GOOD ANYWAY.
Honesty and frankness will make you vulnerable.
BE HONEST AND FRANK ANYWAY.
What you spend years building may be destroyed overnight.
BUILD ANYWAY.
People really need help but may attack you if you help them.
HELP PEOPLE ANYWAY.
Give the world the best you have and you'll get kicked in the teeth.
GIVE THE WORLD THE BEST YOU'VE GOT ANYWAY.

There is a saying in sports that a team must play well enough to outperform the referees. What this means is that sometimes the calls don't go your way. A championship team expects this and determines to play well enough to compensate for two or three unfair calls. This is how any of us aspiring to become Performers must behave. We must prepare and perform enough to outrun any unfair setbacks that come up along the way.

Life is not fair, and sooner or later that is true for everyone. Performers know this and win anyway.

Performers Know There Will Always Be Critics

On the journey to success, the loudest sound a Performer may hear is the cries of critics. Critics are numerous and constant. They pop out of the woodwork anytime somebody tries to do anything worthwhile. Performers know this and learn to ignore their critics while remaining true to their vision and purpose. As it has been said, the surest way to failure is to try to please everyone.

> *Learning to become a Performer must involve the growing of thick skin.*

Sam Walton, billionaire founder of Wal-Mart, said, "Swim up stream. Go the other way. Ignore the conventional wisdom. But be prepared for a lot of folks to wave you down and tell you you're headed the wrong way."

Learning to become a Performer must involve the growing of thick skin. Great leaders throughout history posted their timeless achievements amidst and despite thunderous criticism, not in the absence of it.

Abraham Lincoln, one of the United States' most esteemed presidents for preserving the Union during the tumultuous Civil War and ending slavery once and for all, is perhaps the best example of grace under fire. Lincoln's election to the presidency precipitated the storm that had been brewing for a long time. Between the time he was elected and the time he took office, seven states left the United States and formed their own country. Lincoln's predecessor had given up hope and did absolutely nothing. Congress was equally stagnant. The new Confederate States of America had quickly seized control of military strongholds and depots in the Southern territory. They controlled nearly the entire Mississippi River and looked poised to attack the almost completely undefended capital city of Washington. The United States Army was tiny and unprepared for war. Threats were made against Lincoln's life, and his inauguration was performed under a cloud of fear. Donald T. Phillips writes in *Lincoln on Leadership,* "The nation was in a crisis more severe and ominous than at any other time in American history . . . and there was no effective leadership anywhere in the government."

Against all this opposition stood Abraham Lincoln, an unknown country lawyer who couldn't even command the respect of his own appointed cabinet. His only political experience consisted of a single term in congress, and even his election to the presidency occurred with a minority of the popular vote.

President Lincoln persevered through some of the most hostile criticism anyone could imagine, under grave circumstances and amidst enormous personal suffering (brought on by the death of his son). But he didn't seek approval from others or the adulation of the crowd. He focused on his one great goal of preserving the Union and relied upon the fact that "right makes might."

To a lesser degree, Performers in any field must learn these same lessons, realizing that the one who says it can't be done should never stand in the way of the one doing it. Remember, no one ever does anything worthwhile for which they are not criticized.

Perhaps Confederate general Robert E. Lee said it the most succinctly: "It is better to go steadily in the discharge of duty to the best of our ability, leaving all else to the calmer judgment of the future and to a kinder Province."

Performers Know There Will Always Be Strong Adversaries

The competition never sleeps, and that is why winning is like chasing a moving target. Performers must develop the maturity to realize that there will always be a rival in opposition to their achievements. This rival may appear in the form of healthy competition for a certain position or achievement, or it may be someone committed to opposing your success and working to ensure your failure. But no matter what the form, greatness is always opposed. Performers know this and use the opposition to better themselves. As an Olympic athlete once said, "The competition is only there to keep me honest, ensuring that I extract the optimum performance from myself."

Performers Understand that Breaks Will Come to Those Who Prepare

Baseball great Hank Aaron once said, "In playing ball, or in life, a person occasionally gets the opportunity to do something great. When that time comes, only two things matter: Being prepared to seize the moment and having the courage to take your best swing."

> **Success comes when opportunity and preparedness meet.**

Pat Summitt, legendary coach of the University of Tennessee Lady Volunteers basketball team, notes that "everybody wants to win. But very few people are willing to *prepare* to win. There is not much you can control in this life. But how hard you work is within your control." Success comes when opportunity and preparedness meet. It's what a person does when there are no outward results that determines the height of his or her greatness later. A performer learns to prepare when there is no applause or positive feedback, relying on that day when the opportunity will come to make all the hard work pay off. Christian Laettner, who played basketball under Coach Mike Krzyzewski, or "Coach K," at Duke University, said, "We won championships at Duke because of what happened behind closed doors." Coach John Wooden said, "You must . . . realize that [your] goal will be simply a by-product of all the hard work and good thinking you do along the way—your preparation. The preparation is where success is truly found." According to astronaut John Glenn, "The greatest antidote to worry, whether you're getting ready for space flight or facing a problem of daily life, is preparation. The more you try to envision what might happen and what your best response and options are, the more you are able to calm your fears about the future."

The mark of a true Performer is perhaps best summarized by the lyrics in an old rock song: "When my ship rolls in I'll be ready."

Performers Know that Attitude Conquers Circumstances

Attitude is paramount to understanding the performance of a leader. Zig Ziglar tells us, "Your attitude, not your aptitude, will determine your altitude." Michel de Montaigne said, "A man is not hurt so much by what happens, as by his opinion of what happens." A leader's attitude is critical to his success.

One of the most demanding training programs to be found in the entire United States military is the Basic Underwater Demolition—Sea, Air, Land, or BUD/SEAL qualification conducted in Coronado, California. It is grueling, tough, and very physically demanding. Many candidates drop out before completion. Interestingly, they do not fail because of lack of physical conditioning or ability. According to one of the program's instructors, "The attitude of a trainee has as much to do with his success at Coronado as his physical ability. It's not physical toughness, it's mental toughness. Fitness is a by-product of personal integrity." It seems that even if the body is capable, the attitude is still the determining factor.

One of the keys to having and maintaining a positive attitude is to focus only upon what one can control. As the saying goes, "There is no bad weather, just bad clothing!"

Performers Understand that Desire Trumps Talent

Each individual comes into the world with a unique set of circumstances. Family lives, education, relationships, and physical characteristics are all different. Talent levels and opportunities vary. People are not the same in all things, but results can be equalized with effort. Making the very most of what we have is success, and doing that springs from the well of desire.

Seneca, the Roman moralist, philosopher, and politician, said,

"The greater part of progress is the desire for progress." Performers know that desire eventually trumps talent, every time. A person can't change his native abilities, but he can certainly control how he uses what he has.

Performers Can Never Be Satisfied

The Bible says, "The prosperity of fools shall destroy them" (Proverbs 1:32). As mentioned before, the very support structure of leadership is hunger: a strong productive desire to affect the status quo in a positive way. Ambition dies when satisfaction becomes too pervasive. As leaders perform and begin bringing their vision to reality, there will always be the temptation to become complacent or lazy, to give in to the satisfaction of a job well done. Performers are on guard against this and strive to maintain their hunger and grow their vision even bigger.

> "Hunger not for success, but for excellence."

We can never be perfect, but we must never cease wanting to be. If leaders truly hunger for excellence, their quest will never be complete and they will never become too satisfied. Excellence can always be more excellent. As the saying goes, "If what you did yesterday still looks pretty big to you, then you haven't done enough today."

Performers Know There Is Power in Belief

Anton Chekhov said, "Man is what he believes." John Stuart Mill wrote, "One person with a belief is equal to a force of ninety-nine who have only interests." In the book *What to Say When You Talk to Your Self*, author Shad Helmstetter tells us, "The brain simply believes what you tell it most. Whatever thoughts you have programmed into yourself, or have allowed others to program into you, are affecting, directing, or controlling everything about you." There seems to be a natural tendency for much of this "programming" to be negative in nature. Helmstetter continues, "If we grew up in fairly average, reasonably positive homes, we were told 'No!' or what we could not do, more than 148,000 times! As much as seventy-five percent or more of everything that is recorded and stored in our subconscious minds is counterproductive and works against us—in short, we are programmed *not* to succeed!" Perhaps this is why so many people never develop as leaders and find success elusive. What we believe will happen and what actually does happen is largely one and the same. There is a self-fulfilling quantity to both worry and optimism. Winners choose the power of belief in a positive outcome. David Schwartz says, "Believe, really believe you can succeed, and you will."

The story is told of a Russian schoolboy who had a warm relationship with his father. As an expression of his love, the father would regularly tell the boy, "I'll always be there for you, son." Then the day came when the largest earthquake ever to hit Asia struck and crumbled most of the town's buildings to the ground. Included in the destruction was the school the boy was attending. For days the father dug through the rubble using nothing but his bare hands. He did most of the digging alone, with only an occasional passerby lending aid. "Give it up," said those who saw the desperate father. "He's gone." But the father held firm to his belief that he would find his son alive. Finally, the boy was pulled from the wreckage—alive—along with several other children from the class who had believed the boy's repeated urgings: "My father will come. Believe me, he will come. He said he will always be there for me, and he will come!" The boy and his friends stayed alive without food and water for several days, surviving on the sole belief that they would be rescued. The boy's father performed a near-miraculous physical feat by believing that he would find his boy still alive.

There is power in belief. It is a fact that beliefs control realities. Belief compels leaders to reach for what may seem unattainable to

> "Believe, really believe you can succeed, and you will."

others. It allows people to push beyond the seemingly impossible. It pulls people through when all the evidence would suggest they should quit. Performers learn to foster a strong set of beliefs that enable them to do what they do. Good things normally occur to those who believe that they will!

Actions or the "Science" of Performing

After a firm understanding of the presuppositions growing leaders must comprehend to become Performers, it is appropriate to delve into the *actions* of performing, or the "science" side of what becoming a Performer is all about.

Performers Work as Part of an Overall Team

Leaders at Level 2 must recognize that they will accomplish more by being part of an overall team than they ever could on their own. Ray Kroc, founder of McDonald's Corporation, said, "None of us is as important as all of us." And then there is the famous acronym: TEAM, Together Everyone Achieves More. Leaders learning to perform must realize that they are a cog in a bigger wheel, and they should direct their efforts in whatever ways are necessary to make that wheel spin the way it was intended. After helping the New England Patriots NFL football team win its third AFC Championship in four years, linebacker Ted Johnson commented, "We've created a culture of winning; it starts from our owner . . . and it just permeates throughout the whole organization. You just can't put enough emphasis on character of guys. Our guys believe in each other, they believe in their abilities, and they're willing to sacrifice for the greater good." That's how winners function as part of a team, and that's how teams win.

Performers Edify the Organization's Leadership

Along with realizing their role in the larger team structure, leaders becoming Performers should edify the leadership of the organization. What does it mean to edify? In this usage it means to "lift others up" through words and respect. This doesn't mean some strange sort of worship or idolatry. Edification of the leaders in authority above him is simply how a Performer amplifies his work and strengthens the bonds of the overall team. It is also how he shows respect. Edification can be done by praising with words, showing respect through actions, and taking care to advertise the accomplishments of the leadership. This is important because it sets the stage for how the developing leader will be treated by his followers as he ascends the Levels of Influence on his own journey. Edification goes back to the Golden Rule: "Do unto others as you would have others do unto you." If a developing leader consistently seeks the good in the organization's leadership and amplifies that message, it will come back to him in droves.

Performers Promote the Training System and Learning Environment

Leaders at the Performer Level must also embrace the training system and learning environment of their organization. This means not only taking full advantage of it for themselves, but also becoming promoters of it to others in the organization. In this way, a Performer *amplifies* his energy throughout the organization and empowers others to learn and grow also. Promoting means to help others understand the benefits of something. There is a proper way to do this, and it involves three steps:

1. Announce
2. Explain
3. Promote

Whenever promoting a facet of the training system, leaders should first announce it clearly. Announcements are simply inclusive of all the facts about something, such as the what, when, and where. Next, leaders should explain the event or training aid in enough detail to communicate any background information that will help the listener understand exactly what is being promoted. Finally, leaders should promote by highlighting the relevance of the item for the listener. Remember, the number one thing most people care about when hearing about something new is, What's in it for me? This is where it is helpful if leaders have taken the time to get to know the people around them, as covered previously. In such cases, leaders can promote specifically to the needs and abilities of the listener, thereby ensuring the relevance of the message.

A key to promotion is the concept of "uniqueness." When promoting any facet of the organization, the leader must first ask, What is unique about this? Perhaps it is the first time such an event has been held, or perhaps it is the last. Maybe it is a brand-new training technique but has already received wonderful results. Whatever the case, leaders look for uniqueness before they begin to promote. This adds value to the promotion and increases relevance to the listener.

Leaders understand that the ability to promote effectively is important to empowering the team around them to higher levels of achievement. As this happens, everybody wins.

Performers Follow the Proven Methods

There are certain techniques and strategies for every organization and endeavor that have been proven, over time, to work. Leaders on the track to becoming Performers embrace these proven methods and strive to become experts at them. Their goal is to master these patterns of performance. There is a time and a place for innovation and even radical change, but it is not at this level. If a leader has not proven mastery of the basic strategies and patterns, he has no ground to stand on when attempting to initiate change. In such instances, he will not be taken seriously and his influence will be minimal.

Remember, leadership is influence. If a leader has no record of performance, that leader will have no influence. The quickest, most assured way of gaining that track record of performance is to absolutely master the patterns of success already established

> "When a Gentleman hath learnt how to obey, he will grow very much fitter to command."

in an organization. It should be the goal of every leader striving to become a Performer that the entire organization notices his abilities with the proven patterns. This will give him a platform and the experience to help others accomplish similar results. That is the route to influence. As the Marquis of Halifax wrote in 1693, "When a Gentleman hath learnt how to obey, he will grow very much fitter to command."

Performers Build on Their Basic Strengths

If people are not created equal in all things, then it only follows that people are unequal in different things. This means that some are better in some areas than others. Performers learn to use their strengths to gain success, while working in the background to minimize the shortcomings of their weaknesses. They build on their strengths and starve their weaknesses. Nobody is good at everything, but everyone is good at *something*. Success comes from identifying what your *strength* is and building on it.

Performers Initiate Activity

Leaders absolutely must be self-starters. Personal initiative is not optional for a leader. It is the sole responsibility of a leader to motivate herself. That is why we spent so much time covering the various types of motivation earlier in this book. Leaders must know what makes them tick, and they must wind the mechanisms of that clock on a regular basis. Often, growing leaders ask their mentors if they will do one thing or another to help them stay motivated; a wise mentor will answer that although he may be willing, he knows he would fail miserably. There is no source of external circumstances that can be relied upon to provide consistent motivation to a Performer. It is an internal job. Leaders must embrace this truth and strive daily to motivate themselves to take initiative, be self-starting, and perform. That habit is a sure indicator of a leader who is maturing in the development process.

When it comes to initiative, we like what former prime minister of India Indira Gandhi had to say: "There are two kinds of people: those who do the work and those who take the credit. Try to be in the first group; there is less competition there."

Performers Push to Grow and Improve

No one has ever accomplished great things by babying himself. Along with taking personal initiative, leaders must learn to push themselves beyond the borders of their comfort zone. What is a comfort zone? It is the fictitious area of activity in which a person feels comfortable. It is fictitious because the concept of familiarity is actually being confused with "comfort." A more accurate term would be the *familiar* zone. How many leaders are really *comfortable* in their normal activities? We have already established that would-be leaders start with a discontent with the status quo. The terms *comfort* and *leadership* are at war with one another, so to a leader there can't actually be a *comfort* zone.

This idea of a familiar zone is real. The challenge becomes stepping beyond the familiar or easy. That is the very task of a leader: to take people where, many times, even the leader has never been. To do this, leaders must embrace the idea of being uncomfortable and in unfamiliar territory on a regular basis. When

leaders stop getting outside of their familiar zone, they cease to be leaders.

It is okay and even necessary for a
leader to push himself. Great achievements are always located beyond the
door of inconvenience. The rewards

> *No one has ever accomplished great things by babying himself.*

for achievement hide themselves beyond the borders of the familiar zone, awaiting those with the guts and the discipline to push
hard, experience personal growth, improve, act with courage, and
go places not gone before to claim those rewards as their prize. To
the victor go the spoils. In the world of leadership, the victor is the
one who pushes to grow and improve consistently. Winston
Churchill said, "It is never possible to guarantee success; it is only
possible to deserve it." Performers know this and push themselves
until they know they deserve success.

Performers Become Relatable

Here we see again the importance of the people skills the
leader learned in Level 1: in order to maximize his influence, a
leader must be relatable. This means being likable, being sincere,
and dealing with people in a "low friction" way. People who leave
a trail of broken relationships and hurt feelings or who lash out at
others or act bossy rarely have any real influence with people.
Leaders must take an active interest in others by inquiring, listening, smiling, and caring. These qualities make the leader relatable
to others and build trust—and trust is the foundation of relationships. Only with these bonds can leaders wield any influence in
the lives of others.

Abraham Lincoln was famous for his ability to get along with
others. It was something he actively pursued. In one instance,
after a particularly cantankerous gentleman left the oval office,
President Lincoln said, "I don't like that man. I'm going to have

to get to know him better." That's the attitude that makes a leader relatable.

Performers Become Believable and Demonstrate Conviction

Credibility is the currency of leadership. Leaders gain credibility with their organizations by fostering trust and demonstrating a history of performance. But they also do it through their conviction. In many cases the leader's vision will be larger and farther reaching than that held by most of the organization. For this reason it may be difficult for followers to believe in the vision of the leader; it is beyond their grasp. Belief in the vision is important for the organization, but it can come later. What must happen first is that the people believe in the leader. People must first buy in to the leader

> *It is not important that people believe in the vision, but they must believe the leader believes in it!*

before they buy in to the vision. It is not important that people believe in the vision, but they must believe the leader believes in it! Followers can run on the leader's conviction until they gain their own. This applies across all levels of influence. Leaders must demonstrate conviction with both words and actions. As the saying goes, "Words become credible by deed."

Performers Maintain a Positive Attitude

The mark of a great Performer is a positive attitude. Proper attitude can help leaders accomplish things that otherwise would appear impossible. Sometimes things go well, sometimes they don't. Mature leaders understand that it is not what happens to them, but how they respond that counts. Stephen Covey, author of *The Seven Habits of Highly Effective People*, explains that between stimulus and response we have a choice of how we are going to react. We are response-able, i.e., responsible. That is where good attitudes come from: knowing we have a choice in the matter and making the mature choice to maintain a cheery outlook no matter what happens.

One reason attitude is so important is because it is contagious. Have you ever known someone who has a sour disposition to walk into a room and bring everybody down? They are called "sunshine people"—the room brightens when they leave! Or, conversely, have you ever noticed how contagious a smile can be? We all know people who smile readily and just always seem to be cheery. Whether uplifting or discouraging, attitudes are contagious—and a positive attitude is much more productive than a negative one.

Another reason attitudes of leaders are so important is because they are of a self-fulfilling nature. There is a gravestone in England that reads, SEE, I TOLD YOU I WAS SICK. Attitudes are like that. They tend to produce what we command of them. We don't get what we want, and we don't get what we deserve, but we usually get what we expect. Attitude plays a big part in determining what we expect to happen.

The story is told of two duck hunters who went out in a boat early one morning. After shooting the first duck, one of the hunters, who had brought along his dog, sent the dog to fetch the duck. The dog leaped from the boat, ran across the surface of the water, and retrieved the duck. The dog's owner smiled with pride, but the other man said nothing. A while later another duck was shot. Again the dog scampered across the water to retrieve it. And again the second man was silent. Finally, the dog's owner said, "Did you notice anything particular about my new dog?" To which the second man replied, "Yes, he can't swim!" It seems some people can find the negative in any situation. Some people aren't happy unless they are unhappy. And bad attitudes are notoriously missed in self-assessments. Most people think they have a positive attitude, but so few people actually do. It is much more natural to criticize, condemn, and complain. Performers take an honest look at themselves and actively work to find the best in any situation.

Attitude, like many of the other actions of a Performer, is actually a *discipline*.

People with positive attitudes just simply seem to outperform people with poor attitudes. For no other reason than pragmatism, leaders should work to keep their attitudes high, because sooner or later the man who wins is the man who thinks he can.

Performers Give Their Best in Every Situation

It is a natural tendency to blame performance in life on circumstances. "I had a bad childhood," says one. "I've been discriminated against," says another. "I wasn't given the talents those others have." These excuses are all too common. Performers know that it is not what happens, but how they *respond*, that leads to greatness. Champions are people who make the best of their circumstances. It doesn't matter where you start; it matters how you finish. Talent and wealth and connections and luck can certainly give a person a head start, but almost always the victory goes to the most determined and committed. President Calvin Coolidge said it best:

> Press on.
> Nothing in the world can take the place of persistence.
> Talent will not.
> Nothing is more common than unsuccessful men with talent.
> Genius will not.
> Unrewarded genius is almost a proverb.
> Education alone will not.
> The world is full of educated derelicts.
> Persistence and determination alone are omnipotent.

Winners know that adversity becomes the canvas on which they paint their achievement.

Performers Focus on Priorities

As detailed in the Cycle of Achievement, productivity comes from focus. Alexander Graham Bell said, "Concentrate all your thoughts upon the work at hand. The sun's rays do not burn until brought to a focus." Performers often accomplish so much because they bring all their energies to bear upon a single point of interest. Sooner or later, obstacles and roadblocks have to crumble under the intensified weight of focused energy.

Lou Holtz represents this principle with the acronym WIN, which stands for What's Important Now? Performers must keep that question in mind so they can focus their energies on the one most important thing at a given moment. Most people try to do too much with too little focus and end up accomplishing next to nothing. Performers focus on priorities and concentrate their energies on the best things to do, leaving the good things for another time.

> *"There is no try, only do."*

Performers Get Results (Execute)

All of these attributes of leaders in the performance stage are important, but everything eventually comes down to results. Performers must shore up their resources and apply their learning so that they generate fruit for their labors. There are very few things that command respect the way results do. Leaders must be effective. As our friend Larry Van BusKirk says, "It can't be a try." Or as the character Yoda from the *Star Wars* movies said, "There is no try, only do."

You can always tell the real leaders because their teams consistently turn in superior performances. Leaders must avoid the pitfalls of appearing busy but having little to show for it, hoping somehow to act and look the part but never quite delivering the goods.

One of the authors (Chris) owned a dog named Mindy, a cute

little cocker spaniel–poodle mix. She was a delightful dog except for one remarkable behavior: she would not come when called. Instead, she would wriggle around on the ground making all sorts of commotion, usually punctuating her neurotic behavior with urination. Her tail would wag, her head would shake, her paws would churn at the ground, and she would turn repeatedly in circles, but she would not come. Some would-be leaders behave nearly this way. When called upon to perform they make all sorts of commotion, hoping to demonstrate their good intentions. They shake and shimmy and make all of the right noises, but when all is said and done there is a lot more said than done.

Leaders cannot "Mindy" around; they must perform. They must generate results. Author James A. Autry said the key comment is, "I see you've been busy. Now tell me what you've accomplished." This is especially important at this stage in the Levels of Influence. If a leader does not learn to accomplish goals at this level, there will be no advancement to the next and no increase in influence.

Performers Ignore Their Press Clippings

A close cousin to complacency is arrogance. As leaders perform and success follows, there will be recognition and rewards. It is important not to get too puffed up with one's success or "read the press clippings." Basketball great Michael Jordan won just about everything possible in the National Basketball League, but found ways to set new personal and team goals to keep himself motivated and on the path to continual improvement, even after becoming one of the world's most famous personalities and making millions upon millions of dollars. Performers know that they are no better than anybody else and they guard against the pitfalls of ego and arrogance. This is most easily done by remembering that the opportunities and abilities to perform in one's field are gifts from God.

Such an outlook not only prevents arrogance but also fosters a spirit of gratefulness.

Influence by Performing: Tom Brady
"From Passed-Over to MVP"

It was early fall of the year 2001. The New England Patriots NFL football team was captained by star quarterback Drew Bledsoe, a much acclaimed and in-command "franchise" player. But the team was a lackluster performer at best. *Sports Illustrated* predicted they would finish last that year in their division (AFC East). Then, to make matters worse, during the second game of the season, Drew Bledsoe landed on the turf writhing in pain. He had suffered a chest injury that would take him out for many games and possibly the whole season. Things had gone from bad to worse. An already poor team had lost its star. The Patriots were off to a 0–2 start, and fans had little faith in the young quarterback who jogged out onto the field to replace Bledsoe. Tom Brady was in only his second year as a pro and had thrown only three passes in regulation play. He was young and inexperienced.

Years earlier, however, the even younger Tom Brady had been busy learning how to become a Performer. Everything in his life was a competition, and he admits that he was a sore loser. He decided that the best way to learn to cope with losing was to avoid it, and seek ways to win. "Growing up, I can remember kids who were faster than me and kids who were better jumpers than me. I wasn't going to beat them on pure athletic ability. So I found other ways," he said. After receiving a football scholarship to play for the University of Michigan Wolverines, he sat on the bench for three years. In 1998 he got his chance, and led the team to a 10–3 finish and a victory in the Citrus Bowl, but was forced to split time the following season with rising sophomore star Drew Henson, who impressed the coaches with his flashier style of play. Brady wasn't too happy with this new arrangement, but he learned the valuable lesson that you can't rest on past performance. Realizing that he couldn't control Drew Henson or the decisions of the coaches, he redoubled his efforts, worked extremely hard, and won back his starting position midway through the season, leading the team to another bowl game victory.

The NFL draft was next. According to sportswriter Jennifer Allen, "One national reporter projected that Brady had 'a slightly better than 50-50 chance to make the roster of an NFL team.' " Brady was chosen as the 199th pick, taken in the sixth round. That means that *all* the teams in the NFL passed on him at least five times each. The day after the draft, the *Boston Globe* called Brady a "pocket passer who will compete for a practice squad spot." *Sports Illustrated* said, "Brady wasn't expected to make any important contributions to the offense." Brady was positioned as the fourth-string quarterback, officially classified as "inactive" for sixteen games. Inactive players don't dress for the games, and spend them as fans watching the team.

But Tom Brady had fought his way from the bottom before, while at Michigan, and knew exactly what to do. Allen said, "As [Brady] had done all his life, he kept working hard. . . . He attended every team workout, went on a weight-training program, and gained 30 pounds. At night, he read the playbook, studied the playbook, and memorized the playbook. More than anything, he practiced. He practiced his five-step drop on the field, he studied it on film, and then, at nights, he practiced it in his apartment." According to *Sports Illustrated*, "Brady worked hard to find an edge that would force the coaching staff to notice him. He learned the Patriot playbook inside and out and strived for perfection whenever he touched the ball in practice. Even when he was on the second or third team, he was still getting angry at himself for not making plays." Due largely to this attitude, Brady was named the second-string quarterback for the 2001 season. Because the starter

Drew Bledsoe was so durable, having missed only six games to injury in eight NFL seasons, nobody expected Brady to see much playing time. But when Bledsoe went down, Brady was ready.

In Brady's first game as a starter he led the Patriots to a 44–13 victory. Two weeks later he turned in his first 300-yard passing game while calmly leading the Patriots to an overtime win. The Patriots ended the regular season 11–3 with Brady as a starter. Then in Super Bowl XXXVI, with a hundred million fans watching and 1:21 left to play, Brady led the offense 53 yards for the winning field goal. His poise and ability to perform under pressure awarded him the Super Bowl Most Valuable Player trophy, making him the youngest player ever to attain those honors, at the age of twenty-four.

Even with these accomplishments, however, Brady had his critics. They said the Patriots had the best coach in the league with Bill Belichick. They said the team had one of the best offensive lines in all of football, which would make any quarterback look good. Many said that Drew Bledsoe was still a better quarterback and would have done the same or more if healthy. When in the 2002 season the Patriots traded Drew Bledsoe and made Brady their starting quarterback, the Patriots had a difficult year, not even making it to the playoffs and surrendering their Super Bowl title without a fight.

In true form, however, Brady led the Patriots back. They won fifteen straight games in the 2003 season, including Super Bowl XXXVIII. Again, Tom Brady was named Super Bowl MVP. Their winning streak extended into the 2004 season and set a new NFL record at 21 consecutive wins. Then Brady led the Patriots to a third Super Bowl victory in four years, making the Patriots only the second team in NFL history to accomplish that feat. Then, as a starting quarterback, Brady chalked up a postseason record of 9–0, tying the record set by Hall of Fame legend Bart Starr.

Brady had undeniably become a Performer. Zach Thomas of

the Miami Dolphins said, "I think he's one of the most underrated guys at the position, even though he has [three] Super Bowl rings," and *Monday Night Football*'s John Madden agreed, saying, "I think he is still underrated."

Tom Brady personifies what it means to become a Performer. At first, he didn't start out a champion and he was often made to feel second best, and in fact was forced to play second string! But despite critics and strong adversaries, he maintained a good attitude and focused only on what he could control, working harder and harder. When the coaches had Tom Brady playing a back-bench role on the team, he focused not on their decisions or the performance of the other players competing for the position, but upon what he himself could do about changing the situation.

His preparation and attitude paid off when his big chances came (*Your break will come if you prepare*), and therefore he was able to capitalize beautifully on them. Even after experiencing massive success by anyone's standards, Tom Brady refused to get arrogant (*Don't read your press clippings.*) and continued to *focus* on the challenges ahead. When the pressure of national attention, big games, or tight scores mounted, Brady refused to crack because he had built up such a massive belief in himself and his abilities through the "fiery furnace" of overcoming struggles. He had proven to himself that he could succeed if he would just follow the rules of becoming a Performer. That is exactly what he did!

Summary

Would-be leaders making their way up the Five Levels of Influence and becoming Performers (Level 2 Leaders) will embody each of the steps in this chapter while continuing to follow the principles of Learning we outlined in Level 1.

Becoming a Performer is a prerequisite to becoming a leader. *Again, becoming a Performer* must *happen before one can become a real*

Leader. It is performance that gives the budding leader credibility and influence and the ability actually to begin the calling of a leader—which is, of course, leading! Many, many would-be leaders miss this crucial step of becoming a Performer themselves. They assume that if they are given a position or act with authority, people will follow them. What they fail to realize is that they are then managing, not leading. There is a world of difference between the two. Only when one becomes an obvious Performer do others give one permission to truly Lead. Then it's time for Level 3.

CHAPTER 8

The Third Level of Influence: Leading

Being a general calls for talents different than those of a soldier.

—Titus Livy

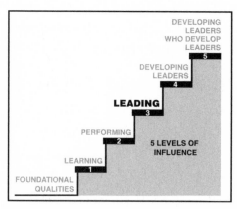

So far we have discussed ways a leader grows personally; now it is time to deal specifically with the budding leader's ability to increase in influence through the leadership of other people. The leader thus far has made Learning a habit, has gained valuable experience becoming a high Performer, and is now ready to take responsibility for the Leadership of others. At this level, the group grows when and because the Leader is present. When capitalized, the term "Leader" will refer to a Level 3 Leader.

The soccer player from the previous two chapters is now becoming an on-field Leader of the other players. She is named team captain, and, while playing the game herself, also calls plays and directs activities.

Presuppositions or the "Art" of Leading

Just as with the previous step of becoming a Performer, becoming a Leader requires a certain mind-set. It starts with the correct presuppositions or mentalities. Without an understanding of the thought processes upon which leadership of others is based, a leader will have trouble implementing the correct actions of leadership. This is because leadership itself is a perspective; it is the lens through which a person views the world. Leaders learn to see things a certain way, from a certain vantage point, so they can take responsibility for achievement through the efforts of a unified group of people. J. Robert Clinton said, "The difference between leaders and followers is perspective. The difference between leaders and effective leaders is better perspective. Effective leaders have better perspective." How a leader sees things, his or her perspective, is critical, and it is based upon his or her presuppositions.

Leaders Understand that Results Come Through Team Effort

Leadership is how a Performer extends his or her ability through the efforts of others, to the betterment of everyone involved. Let's look again at the acronym TEAM: Together Everyone Achieves More. Level 3 Leaders think this way as a matter of course. In every situation the leader thinks in terms of "team" efforts and what resources he or she can pull together to get the job done. At Level 3, the working concept is no longer what the individual can do, but rather what a *team* of individuals can do.

This concept could be called "leverage." To explore this further, let's return to the equation we used in an earlier chapter:

$$Work = Force \times Distance$$

Or, as we modified it:

$$Influence = Effort \times Scope$$

The equation reveals that, assuming leaders have maximized their effort, the only remaining way to increase Influence is through increasing Scope. Webster defines leverage as the action of a lever or the mechanical advantage gained by it. It can be seen that a leader's team is his lever. There is a mechanical advantage gained by a leader orchestrating the efforts of a group of people to accomplish some larger task. When this is done properly, leaders amplify the power of individuals beyond the sum of the parts. As the saying goes, individuals can flourish but teams explode. Leverage is the ability to put in X amount of work but receive back several times X.

Consider again Bill Gates, billionaire founder of Microsoft Corporation and one of the world's richest individuals. How did Bill Gates's ideas for software for computers explode into such a large industry and an enormous fortune? There are many answers to this, of course, but one that can describe it as well as any is the concept of leverage. Software is nothing more than a computer program. It can be stored on various forms of media. When Microsoft creates a new software product, for example the latest version of Windows, they then sell that product to customers. They can transfer that computer program to customers in many ways: on an optical disc or even downloaded electronically over the Internet.

The cost of the actual product transferred to the customer is very little. In the case of an optical disc it may be only a few dollars; in the case of an Internet download, radically less. What is being paid for is not the medium of transfer but the computer program itself. That program was constructed one time and then copied millions of times. A term that describes this multiplication of results is *duplication*. A finished product is very cheaply duplicated over and over. That's leverage. It may very well be one of the simplest and purest forms of duplication ever devised. That largely explains the enormous multiplier on Microsoft's income stream. Build a program once, duplicate it cheaply, and sell it millions of times. It could be said that Bill Gates and Microsoft leverage their expertise across millions of customers (and vigorously protect it with copyright laws, we might add). This is well beyond what Gates and his employees could do individually. For such enormous impact, they have to use the power of leverage.

Leadership works the same way. Leadership amplifies the reach or scope of a Performer through the joint efforts of other people. Without leadership, a person is limited to his or her own personal performance. We might say that a Level 2 Leader deals in *addition*, while a Level 3 Leader gains the leverage of *multiplication*.

Leaders Understand that People Buy In to the Leader before Anything Else

A critical presupposition all leaders must realize is that followers buy in to the leader before anything else. The vision may be compelling, but is the leader worth following? The rewards may be inspiring, but can the leader be trusted? The environment may be inviting, but does the leader care about his or her people? The resources may be abundant, but does the leader have character? The opportunities may be enormous, but does the leader know what he or she is doing? These are the qualifying questions followers ask subconsciously before giving permission to be led.

Leadership is not a position or title; it is a condition of permission given by followers once they buy in to the leader. Leadership influence, like trust, must be earned and earned continually.

Leaders Understand the Importance of Finding and Developing Good People

Since the whole concept of leadership is the leverage of accomplishment through the collective efforts of a group of people, it stands to reason that the quality of the output will be directly related to the quality of the people involved. As we said earlier,

> *The quality of the output will be directly related to the quality of the people involved.*

finding and developing the *right* people is critical to the success of an endeavor. Leaders know this and focus on surrounding themselves with the best talent available. This is why attracting, training, and retaining people of high caliber is always a major consideration for a leader.

George Barna said, "Every leader has an incomplete set of tools to lead with and must, therefore, know what he can and cannot do. Effective leaders overcome their weaknesses by combining forces with [others] whose strengths compensate for those weaknesses, thereby creating a more complete and powerful mix of gifts and abilities." Finding and equipping others will consume an enormous amount of a leader's time but, as we have seen through the discussion on leverage, it will be more than worth it. Level 3 Leaders are only as good as their people.

Leaders Understand that Dealing with Inadequate Resources Is Common

While it may be important to lead people of the highest quality possible, most Leaders will find themselves severely lacking in this area. One of the realities of leadership is that there are no perfect teams. No matter how much effort and focus a leader puts upon finding and training people, there will always be deficiencies, and many times those deficiencies will be enormous. Additionally, there will often be a severe lack of other resources, too.

The leader who waits for an abundance of resources before setting out to accomplish a task is no leader at all.

Two British generals were conferring during the American Revolutionary War. General James Grant complained of the English army's lack of provisions and thin lines of supply. Commanding General Cornwallis replied, "Let us not dwell on what *should* be, General. Let us use the means we have at hand, and make it so."

In the American Civil War, George B. McClellan was twice made overall commander of the Army of the Potomac, the major fighting force of the "Union." Each time, he did a marvelous job of training the troops and bringing the discipline of a "regular army" to the rank and file, but he was incessantly unready to take action. On the rare occasions when he did confront the Confederate army, he outnumbered them by two-to-one or even three-to-one, but he always found ways to become convinced that the opposite was true. He complained unendingly to President Lincoln that he didn't have enough men, arms, or supplies to conduct a proper campaign. McClellan suffered from an incorrect presupposition of leadership: he mistakenly thought leaders could demand and expect perfect situations before taking action. Reality for a leader is almost always a situation of lack and want. True Leaders understand this and make do the best they can anyway. As the saying goes, "If you wait for all the lights to turn green before you set off on a cross-country trip, you'll never leave."

Leaders Understand that Leadership Is the Limitation

Author Ken Blanchard wrote, "No organization will rise above the passion of the leader." Leaders cannot blame their people, their resources, or their circumstances. The effectiveness of the Leader is the limitation upon the organization.

It has been said that "people have become astute customers of leadership." This means that in this skeptical society people are getting better and better at spotting phonies. Leadership is not something that can be faked, although people frequently attempt it. Perhaps an individual has a title or position, so he thinks that gives him influence over others. Maybe somebody has achieved things in the past and figures those accomplishments provide influence today. While both of these assumptions may be true to some extent, leadership is earned on a continual basis. Followers look around and know who the real Leaders are in any given situation. This is why it is so critical that a leader is both an ongoing Learner and Performer. Learning, growing, and achieving build up a balance in the "bank account of credibility" with followers. The more a leader leads and the better his or her leadership, the higher the caliber of the followers he or she attracts and the better they perform. The better they perform, the better results the organization achieves. Through this process, the leader develops his or her people to grow personally and increase their personal effectiveness.

Leaders are constantly asking themselves if their teams are getting results. They face brutal reality and make an honest assessment of how their team is doing and, therefore, how they as the Leader are doing. The measure of a Level 3 Leader is the performance of his or her organization and the personal growth of the people involved.

Leaders Understand the Impact of Their Actions on the Organization

Leaders at this Level must be cognizant that their every action has a reaction. There are many connection points to the organization when a Leader is responsible for a group of people. Selfishness, pettiness, and similar malfunctions of a Leader will stop his or her progress cold. Everything a Leader does is amplified now because he does it with and

> **Leadership is about service to others.**

through his people. The ability to think in terms of a bigger picture and live by priorities is critical. At this Level, good judgment and a positive attitude pay big dividends.

Leaders Understand that Leadership Is about Sacrifice

Leadership is not a bed of roses. It is not something to be sought after for the purpose of perks and privilege. Leadership is about service to others. Leadership is a responsibility that demands self-discipline and sacrifice. As a matter of fact, the higher a leader rises, the less tolerance there is for error. As soon as a person becomes responsible for leading others, his or her own walk comes under scrutiny. Followers are checking all the time to see if the leader is "walking the walk" or just "talking the talk." It seems that the higher the leader rises, the more his or her personal freedoms are limited. Failings that may have been ignored at lower levels become poison once someone starts to Lead. This is because everything a Leader does is amplified through his or her organization, and because now the Leader is not just dealing with his or her own life, but also the lives of others. This is a great responsibility.

There are definitely perks and privileges that come with successful leadership, and they are enjoyable and flattering. But these rewards are not the purpose of leadership; they are merely the side benefits. A Level 3 Leader will sacrifice personal desires for the good of the vision and the team. As a Leader puts his or her self-interests aside, learns to serve others and work toward the vision, and sacrifices for a purpose and a cause greater than himself, the rewards go beyond mere perks and trappings of success. The most important rewards become the satisfaction of seeing other people's lives enriched and the vision accomplished. Such deep and truly meaningful rewards make all the sacrifice worth it.

Leaders Understand that a Leader's Job Is Never Done

Leadership is not a "nine-to-five" operation. It does not neatly pack itself into a schedule. Leadership requires constancy and diligence and continual pondering. At no point in the leadership journey does a leader have the luxury of sitting back and thinking "I've arrived" or "I've got it all under control." The moment that happens, and maybe even sooner, the leader will be run over by problems or competition or both. There will always be new challenges and competitors and obstacles and opportunities. Nothing stands still, and leadership greatness is certainly no exception.

> *Great Leaders learn to find a defeat in every victory and a victory in every defeat.*

Great Leaders learn to find a defeat in every victory and a victory in every defeat. What does this mean? First of all, no matter how well a leader and his or her organization perform, there is always room for improvement. Even if every possible award has been won, the statistics will still reveal ways the team could have performed better. This attitude keeps leaders sharp and away from the dangerous Ditch of Complacency. On the other hand, sometimes leaders suffer through defeat after defeat. During those times—and they are likely to come sooner or later—great leaders look for signs of good in an otherwise bleak landscape. Even if it was your organization's worst year in history, there will be something in the data to celebrate and build upon. This attitude keeps a leader out of the Ditch of Discouragement and Despondency.

Actions or the "Science" of Leading

With these presuppositions in mind, it is appropriate to explore what leaders actually do at this Third Level of Influence. That's what the "science" side of leadership is all about.

Leaders Model the Way

Leaders set the example. Authors Kouzes and Posner wrote, "People don't follow your technique—they follow you." To harness the collective energies of a group of people effectively, one must first model the way. There is no shortcut here. Of all the action steps or "science" of leadership that follow, none of it matters if the master copy is not worth duplicating. Level 3 Leaders know this and work hard on their own example.

One question to ask yourself is this: Would I want an entire organization filled with people just like me? If the answer is yes, then you are setting a good example and modeling the way (or are terribly self-deceived).

Leaders Compel Individuals to Perform

A major job of a Level 3 Leader is to inspire others to perform and achieve results. Elmer L. Towns observes, "People follow a leader who gives compelling reasons to reach the objective." Level 3 Leaders know that people will not do what the leader expects, but rather what the leader inspects. The things that get accomplished are the things that get rewarded. Leaders therefore must reward the right activities and get in the habit of "catching their people in the act of doing something right." Outstanding performance must be recognized and rewarded, and this should be done publicly. This communicates a standard to the rest of the organization for which others can strive, and motivates the star performers to reach even greater heights.

> The things that get accomplished are the things that get rewarded.

In *Leadership Lessons from General Ulysses S. Grant*, Al Kaltman writes, "The superior leader knows that the key to success is his or her ability to attract and retain good people and get them to work well together as a team." This is precisely how a Leader increases his or her influence: by inspiring people to work in the same direction, function as a team, and achieve great things together.

An old fable tells of the farmer whose mules pulled a man's truck from the ditch. It was a big truck, the cross-country type, complete with sleeper and fuzzy dice.

"How much can one of those pull?" asked the truck driver, sizing up the farmer's two scrawny-looking mules.

" 'Bout ten tons each," said the farmer.

"But my truck weighs at least three times that," the truck driver said.

"Doesn't matter what they can pull separately," answered the farmer. "It only matters what they can pull *together*."

That's the power of a team. Good leaders compel people to work together and thereby amplify the efforts to the point where the whole is greater than the sum of the parts.

Leaders Coach Others

As we said before, leaders function as coaches. Coaching involves increasing the performance of one's individual team members and getting them to work together effectively.

Leaders at this Level of Influence are responsible and qualified to coach those at the previous two levels. This is one of the reasons it is so important for a leader to master each of the previous Levels of Influence. A leader doesn't really know how well he knows something until he tries to teach it.

Leaders Become Servants

In *The Servant Leader*, authors Ken Blanchard and Phil Hodges tell us, "Leadership is first a matter of the heart. Whenever we have an opportunity or responsibility to influence the thinking and the behavior of others, the first choice we are called to make is whether to see the moment through the eyes of self-interest or for the benefit of those we are leading."

Leaders must learn that to lead means to serve. Leadership is not about position or perks or status. It is not about power or wealth. It is about service to others expanded through the coordinated efforts of people. The single most effective way for a leader to get the most out of his organization is to serve its people.

> *"You can be a servant and not a leader. You can be a leader and not a servant, though not much of a leader."*

Robert Dickie, our friend and pastor of Berean Baptist Church for twenty-three years, says, "You can be a servant and not a leader. You can be a leader and not a servant, though not much of a leader. A true servant leader can answer 'yes' to the following seven questions regarding servant leadership. Do people on your team:

1. Believe that you are willing to sacrifice your own self-interest for the good of the team?
2. Believe that you want to hear their ideas and will value them?
3. Believe that you will understand what is happening in their lives and how it affects them?
4. Come to you when the chips are down or when something traumatic has happened in their lives?
5. Believe you are seeking to make a positive difference in their lives, and in the world?
6. Believe that you are committed to helping them develop and grow?
7. Feel a strong sense of community in the organization that you lead?"

Affirmative answers to these questions demonstrate that the leader is serving his team. By doing the things discussed here, a Leader shows his love for his team and serves them in their efforts to perform. By serving others, a Level 3 Leader maximizes the performance of his or her team.

Leaders Operate as Field Commanders

At Level 3, Leaders exert influence through actually being there in person. They are in the fight with their troops, so to speak, and are on hand to observe and direct activities. They can see changes in conditions and orchestrate accordingly. Their presence is reassuring to their people, and inspiration and vision are given firsthand. At this level the group grows when the leader is present. Effective Third Level Leaders can always be spotted because their groups thrive when they "take the field." It is also here that the leader realizes very quickly that the speed of the group is the speed of the leader. Since the Leader is up close and personal with his people, his performance has a big impact on the overall team's performance. Leadership by example is crucial at Level 3 and above. Personal charisma, people skills, relationships, and rapport make the Level 3 Leader especially effective.

Leaders Orchestrate Activity

Orchestration involves seeing the things that need to be done and coordinating people's efforts in that direction. Leaders must learn to have the right people in the right places. Jim Collins, in his book *Good to Great*, talks about first having the right people on the bus. Then he stresses the importance of having the right people in the right seats on that bus. Both are critical to a Leader's orchestration of his team, and demonstrate once again the importance of a Leader knowing his players. These players have strengths and abilities in certain areas that should be utilized accordingly. This involves how the leader treats each player. Not everyone wants or needs to be treated the same way. Individual attention and knowledge multiplies a Level 3 Leader's effectiveness with his or her team.

Leaders Measure Results

Level 3 is about team *results*, and Level 3 Leaders keep score.

As with any sporting event, there is a scoreboard for an organization (and if there isn't, there should be). Leaders must learn to keep score for what they do so they can accurately measure the performance of their team and therefore glean concrete feedback on their own performance as a Leader.

Without measurement, there can be no portrayal of reality. Without data representing reality, there can be no impetus or plans for improvement. At Level 3, Leaders measure results, confront brutal reality, and take steps toward improvement. Anything less is negligence of duty.

Leaders Solve Problems

Being a problem solver requires courage. Leaders must face challenges head-on and without delay. Problems are much easier to kill when they are small.

Certain situations resemble forest fires and require the leader to throw water on them and douse the flames. Others appear as small embers of possibility and require the leader to pour on some gasoline and incite progress. Successful Third Level Leaders know what is needed and when. They become adept at solving problems and, eventually, even heading problems off at the pass and dousing them before they blossom into full-scale conflagrations.

Leaders Communicate

A leader must be a good communicator. In the military there is a saying used to instruct combat commanders, "Move, shoot, and communicate." It rings true for all leaders. The more aggressive the tasks of the team, the more the leader must communicate. When people are informed, they feel a sense of security and shared ownership in the objectives. When communication is poor, they feel distrust and a lack of closeness. Poor communication breeds friction and trouble. Proper Level 3 Leadership begins, continues, and ends with good communication.

Leadership in Action: George Washington
"The Faithful Servant"

It was December 1777 and the British regular soldiers commanded by General Howe settled into comfortable winter quarters in Philadelphia, a town they had easily captured from the ragtag collection of colonials fighting under George Washington. Philadelphia had been the capital city of the Continental Congress, the governing body administering the "revolution" against the English Crown. The members of the congress had fled the city out of fear for their lives. While they considered themselves patriots, the British government had made it clear that they were to be treated as traitors. As Benjamin Franklin had said, "We must all hang together, or most assuredly, we shall all hang separately."

With the government in flight and fully one-third of the population of the colonies on the side of the British—and with Howe's forces now in possession of both New York and Philadelphia—what would become of the fight for independence? Was the war, which was barely a year and a half old, over?

The members of Congress, many of whom had relocated to York, Pennsylvania, demanded that General Washington retake the city of Philadelphia. But the Continental Army had recently been badly beaten at Brandywine Creek, and then Germantown shortly thereafter. It was worn out, greatly diminished in numbers, and without vital supplies. George Washington told the congress no.

Washington next selected a site called Valley Forge twenty miles northwest of Philadelphia, where he would set up winter camp and at least attempt to keep an eye on the hibernating British. On December 19, 11,000 men, most of whom were between the ages of twenty and twenty-four years old, dragged into camp. The troops were sad, cold, hungry, and largely unclothed. Some had only one shirt. Many had none. Thousands were without hats or coats or shoes or socks. Hundreds more were so sick they couldn't walk and had to be carried. In Washington's famous words, "You might have tracked the army from White Marsh to Valley Forge by the blood of their feet."

Washington immediately set out to provide shelter and accommodations for his men. He formed up hunting parties of able-bodied soldiers, and started everyone upon the construction of wooden huts for housing, partly out of necessity and partly to keep the men occupied. He decided to live in his tent, refusing to inhabit the farmhouse he had commandeered for his own lodging until his men were properly housed. He even ate from the same "fire cake" rations his men suffered through. Then he implemented a daily routine of drill and exercise to rehabilitate his troops and keep them sharp. Eventually, he utilized the many foreign glory-seekers Congress had pawned on him to train and instruct his army in military movements, strategy, and discipline. Of what was supposed to be a fighting army, Washington said, "All I could do under these circumstances was to send out a few light parties to watch and harass the enemy."

Congress seemed unable to understand the hardships the army was enduring, and had no concept of how close they were to having no army at all. Washington wrote to them: "I am now convinced beyond a doubt that unless some great and capital change suddenly takes place, this army must inevitably be reduced to one or other of these three things. Starve, dissolve or disperse, in order to obtain subsistence in the best manner they can." Instead of helping, Congress attacked Washington personally. He was both openly and secretly smeared and discredited. Whispers circulated that other officers would serve more effectively as commanding general. Another general in the cause, General Thomas Conway, even wrote a letter that attacked Washington's character and called for his removal. Most men would have ridden to York immediately to defend themselves, but not George Washington. He would not leave his men in such peril to get involved in defending his own reputation. He would stay where he was needed and do his duty.

Next, Congress ordered Washington to attack British forces up in Canada. Again, much to the dismay of Congress and to the fuel of his adversaries, Washington refused.

As the winter wore on, Washington's men became more disciplined, more skilled, more hardened, and, most of all, more dedicated to their tireless commander in chief who had suffered right alongside them. The men could feel Washington's sincere concern for them. In turn, Washington openly praised his men in letter after letter. "To see men without clothes to cover their nakedness, without blankets to lie on, without shoes . . . and submitting without a murmur, is a proof of patience and obedience which in my opinion can scarce be paralleled," he wrote.

What Washington had realized long before, and what most of the men soon came to understand themselves, was that all they had was each other. Very little help came in from the neighboring towns and colonies. Congress seemed more concerned with anything but the condition of its army. If they were going to pull out of such desperate straits, their only hope was to pull together. For that, true leadership would be required. For that, George Washington was born.

Washington appointed his most trusted general, Nathaniel Greene, as the new quartermaster of his army. Greene immediately took charge and sent foragers as far as some of the southern states to round up food and supplies. Greene managed every penny, replacing the wanton corruption that had permeated the office before him. Finally, local citizens began pitching in too. Then Washington's wife, Martha, showed up and organized all available women to mend and sew clothes. Two thousand men were without shoes, so Washington had them share. Then, he brought in shoemakers to teach soldiers how to make shoes themselves.

According to author Donald T. Phillips in *The Founding Fathers on Leadership*:

> By late March, the once-emaciated soldiers were well clothed, well drilled, and noticeably putting on weight. One officer who kept a journal recorded that "the army grows stronger every day. It increases in numbers and there is a spirit of discipline among the troops that is better than numbers. Each brigade is on parade almost every day for several hours, marching with regularity and exactness." By late May, new recruits were flooding into Valley Forge to become trained members of the now-renewed Continental Army. And by mid-June, Washington had 13,500 men at his disposal.
>
> During the six months at Valley Forge, 3,000 men died of starvation and disease—nearly one in four. Many lost limbs from severe frostbite, and all witnessed their comrades suffer unimaginable hardships. And yet those who survived that fateful winter later pointed to Valley Forge as the turning point of the American Revolution.

When summer came, the British army would find themselves up against a different army than the one they had chased into the Pennsylvania hills the previous winter. It was stronger, better, and bigger than anything they had yet faced in the conflict. And it had been built by the always-attendant care of its leader, George Washington.

Eventually, Congress would get its wish and move back into Philadelphia as the British would lose interest in holding the city to no apparent strategic advantage and at great expense to themselves. But for the Continental Army, there would be many more hardships. The following winter proved even worse than the one spent at Valley Forge. Washington and his troops would experience more losses than anything else in a war that would drag on for years. But Washington, and nearly Washington alone, knew that the fight for independence pivoted entirely on his ability to keep an army in the field. Phillips said of Washington's leadership during Valley Forge, "George Washington had pulled off an amazing turnaround by combining an optimistic attitude with a grounded reality in what the situation was—and what had to be done to rectify it. He was on the spot the entire time, fighting for his people, encouraging them, and living as they lived, walking among them. He listened and acted decisively when it counted. And, more importantly, George Washington never gave up hope."

George Washington is perhaps the best example of a Level 3 Leader history has provided. "It may be doubted whether so small a number of men ever employed so short a space of time with greater and more lasting effects upon the history of the world," said British historian George Trevelyan about George Washington and his Continental Army. Washington recognized the impact of his actions on the bigger picture and used that keen understanding to remain tenacious and inventive in the face of overpowering adversity. He remained present and on the scene (*Model the way*) even when under attack personally, knowing that his attendance, and his only, was required to keep the army together (*Operate as a field commander*). In fact, there was a period of over six years when he didn't see his home at all, and it was never more than a couple days' ride away! (*Leadership requires sacrifice.*) He compelled others to productive action, and gained enormous influence through his constant demonstration of *servant leadership*. He was an effective *orchestrator* of logistics and supply, a calm problem solver, and a disciplined example to his men. He *communicated often* and effectively both in person and through his actions, even reading Thomas Paine's newly printed *Common Sense* aloud to his troops to build their morale.

Realizing that quite possibly he alone was responsible for victory or defeat in the cause of independence (*People buy in to the leader before anything else)*, he took *full responsibility* for the care and training of his army, even when abandoned by his superiors and two-thirds of his country. He molded a rough collection of farmers and merchants (*Leaders will often have to lead with inadequate resources*) into a formidable fighting force, and developed such a bond with his men that his very presence inspired them to bravery. For eight years Washington managed to lead amateur soldiers in a string of losing battles against the world's most powerful and feared military, keeping them together and believing that ultimately, somehow, they could prevail. *That* is leadership.

Historian Page Smith said of Washington, "His genius was the ability to endure, to maintain his equilibrium in the midst of endless frustrations, disappointments, setbacks and defeats." In Washington's own words, "I have been your faithful servant so far as it lay within me to be. I have endured." Level 3 Leaders have much to learn from his enduring example.

Summary

As a leader comes to understand the presuppositions (art) of Level 3 Leadership and habitually execute the actions (science) of Level 3, he or she will rise in influence. Such a Leader will be able to achieve tremendously more significant and sizeable results than anything accomplished by performing personally, while enriching the lives of others in the process. However, at this Third Level of Influence the leverage involved only goes as far as the Leader's personal reach. That influence is a product of the Leader's presence on the scene. But the principles of leadership embodied on the Third Level are amplified in Level 4 as the Leader learns to have influence not just through a band of *followers*, but through the development and effectiveness of other *Leaders*.

CHAPTER 9

The Fourth Level of Influence: Developing Leaders

A leader is best when people barely know he exists. Not so good when people obey and acclaim him. Worse when they despise him. But of a good leader who talks little when his work is done, his aim fulfilled, they will say, "We did it ourselves."

—Lao-tzu (604–531 b.c.)

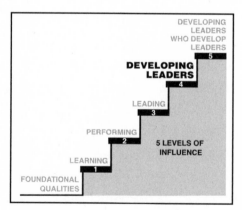

The Fourth of the Five Levels of Influence is Developing Leaders. This level deals with the leader's ability to increase his influence through the development of *other* leaders. The leader continues to Learn (Level 1), Perform (Level 2), and Lead (Level 3), but now develops others who can also thrive at each of those three levels.

Level 4 Leaders become the coaches of Level 3 Leaders and below. John Maxwell said, "Any leader who has only followers around him will be called upon to continually draw on his own resources to get things done. Without other leaders to carry the load, he will become fatigued and burn out." Jack Welch, former chairman of GE, wrote in *Jack: Straight from the Gut*, "We build great people, who then build great products and services," and said of his corporate training, "I wanted it focused on leadership development, not specific functional training." As a matter of fact, he took this task of developing other leaders so far as to say, "We ran the people factory to build great leaders." There is an old saying about prosperity, "If you want one year's prosperity, grow grain, but if you want ten years' prosperity, grow men and women." That's what Level 4 Leaders do, and it has supreme ramifications personally and organizationally. Noel Tichy, author of *The Cycle of Leadership*, writes, "A company's success is directly tied to its ability to create leaders. The companies with the most leaders are the most successful."

A Leader who succeeds in finding and developing other leaders has ascended to the Fourth Level of Influence.

At Level 4 the group grows because the leader has grown *other* Level 3 Leaders. A Level 4 Leader is basically in the business of replacing himself.

Continuing with the example of the soccer player in previous chapters, at Level 4 she has become head coach. Her influence does not stem from her position, though. Rather, it comes from her ability to develop other player-leaders (team captains, etc.) and assistant coaches. Her abilities are employed to develop others into leadership positions within the sport. These individuals seek her mentorship and guidance to aid them in growing their own abilities to lead.

Presuppositions or the "Art" of Leadership Development

As with each of the previous Levels of Influence, there are some vital presuppositions at the step of Developing Other Leaders. Once the presuppositions are right in the mind of the leader, then the correct actions will follow.

There is also a subtle trend at work as we progress upward through the Levels of Influence. The higher a leader goes up the steps, the more important and numerous the *presuppositions*, while at the same time the actual *actions* become smaller and fewer. Said another way, the higher one ascends the Levels, the more "art" and less and less

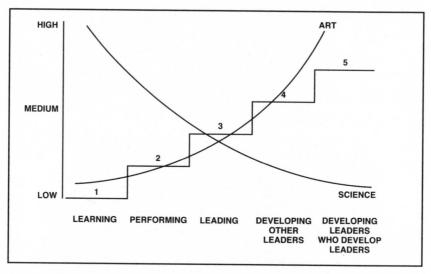

"science" is required. Who one *is* becomes much more important than what one *does*. Don't get us wrong, leaders will be busy and work hard at each of the Five Levels of Influence, but the emphasis of their efforts will change along with their growth in ability.

Level 4 Leaders Know Results Will Come Through the Efforts of Other Leaders

This Fourth Level is significant because it dramatically increases the leader's scope or range. It is where a leader is not content just to lead followers, but also takes the pains to develop other leaders. Let's refer back to the physical equation once again:

$$Influence = Effort \times Scope$$

What we see here is that every time a leader can find and develop another leader who can perform up to the Third Level of Influence, it increases *exponentially* the scope of the original leader. Where a Level 3 Leader benefited from the concepts of leverage in terms of *multiplication* (coordinating the efforts of a unified team of performers), the Level 4 Leader gains the advantages of *exponential* growth (developing other leaders who each deal in *multiplication*).

> *"Obviously, I was surrounding myself with people who were far more talented and gifted than I was."*

Ross Perot, billionaire founder of EDS and Perot Systems, said, "Obviously, I was surrounding myself with people who were far more talented and gifted than I was. This was the secret to EDS's success—the multiplier effect of all this talent." A Level 4 Leader is not concerned with being a star in the organization; he is concerned with developing other stars.

Level 4 Leaders Understand the Power of Duplication

Whereas a Level 3 Leader must be present with his or her team in order to achieve success, Level 4 Leaders get results even when they are not around. This effectiveness obtained through the output of *other leaders* generates a result we call duplication. Duplication is the reason for the exponential growth discussed in the previous paragraph.

Level 4 Leaders confront challenges and opportunities by asking themselves questions such as: Whom have I developed who can handle this? Which of my leaders has a team capable of taking on this task? What have I done or what can I do to help this leader or that leader grow and improve?

Perhaps one of the best examples of the concept of exponential growth through the power of duplication comes from Ray Kroc and the McDonald's franchise system. We mentioned earlier that Kroc's vision extended beyond that of the restaurant's founders. Now it might be helpful to explain the reason *why* Kroc's vision was so large: he understood the power of duplication.

Kroc had become convinced that the system of operation for a profitable fast-food restaurant as developed by the McDonald brothers would work. Kroc's added touch was described by author John Love in *McDonald's: Behind the Arches*:

> The essence of Kroc's unique but amazingly simple franchising philosophy was that a franchising company should not live off the sweat of its franchisees, but should succeed by helping its franchisees succeed. *The genius of Ray Kroc was that he treated his franchisees as equal partners.* [As a result of this] he had something no one else had—franchisees working on his side. What eventually separated McDonald's from the rest of the pack was Kroc's *ability to marshal the efforts of hundreds of other entrepreneurs*—his McDonald's franchisees—to work not merely for their selfish interests but for McDonald's interests. As Ray Kroc saw it, they were one and the same. [Emphasis added]

While most leaders will never experience the power of duplication on the scale Ray Kroc and McDonald's did, the example is clear. Level 4 Leaders are able to align with other leaders in common purpose. Then they develop those leaders to be able to achieve team success even when the Level 4 Leader is not around. The result is productivity that compounds exponentially.

Level 4 Leaders Know that Leaders Have
Strengths in Various Areas

One of the reasons developing *other* leaders works so well is be-cause everybody has different strengths and abilities. Level 4 Lead-ers are not "turf protectors" or "glory hogs" who have to be the best at everything, get the glory for every accomplishment, and be in on every decision. Level 4 Leaders surround themselves with leaders who have strengths in various areas and, in many cases, strengths in areas where the Level 4 Leader is weak. In other words, Level 4 Leaders care more about the vision than their own personal glory. They know that they are not great at everything, so they bring along other leaders who are good in areas where they are not. And they also bring along leaders who are strong where they are strong, and are not intimidated by them.

Level 4 Leaders Know the Vision Must Be Big
Enough for Many Leaders

One of the reasons Level 4 Leaders are able to develop other leaders is that the vision is big enough for all of them. Level 4 Leaders know that the best talent is attracted not solely by high-dollar offers, nor by perks and power, nor privilege, but also by a compelling vision. Level 4 Leaders don't mind surrounding them-selves with talent and helping to grow that talent, because they know there is enough to do for everybody. The accomplishment of the vision has taken priority over smaller, individual goals, which seem petty in comparison to the vision.

Level 4 Leaders Know that Recognition Is the
Most Valuable Motivator

At the Fourth Level of Influence, the leader is widely recog-nized as an expert in his or her field. Level 4 Leaders take some of the "spotlight" shining upon them and share it among the

Performers on their team. They do this loudly and publicly, edifying and recognizing the stars in their organization.

Level 4 Leaders know that the real reason most people in their organizations perform is for the very recognition and praise the Level 4 Leader bestows upon them. Where Level 3 Leaders are happy to receive praise and recognition for their own leadership performance, Level 4 Leaders know that they are not in competition with any of their people and share credit and praise in order to build and develop their leaders. Level 3 Leaders are generally concerned with how much recognition they themselves receive; Level 4 Leaders are focused upon how much recognition they can bestow on others.

Some Level 3 Leaders actually become upset when their own people start matching their performance. Level 4 Leaders never behave that way; instead they get out the checkered flag and wave their people past. That is the signifi-

> *Recognition: Babies cry for it and grown men die for it.*

cant difference between simply *being* a leader oneself and *developing others* into leaders. Level 4 Leaders know the power of recognizing their leaders. They understand how critical it is in the development of others.

Steel magnate Charles Schwab once said, "I consider my ability to arouse enthusiasm among my people the greatest asset I possess, and the way to develop the best that is in a person is by appreciation and encouragement." It must have worked. Schwab became a fabulously wealthy man known for building leadership ability in others.

As the saying goes concerning recognition, "Babies cry for it and grown men die for it." Level 4 Leaders require neither tears nor death before praising their leaders; they know to offer it lavishly.

Actions or the "Science" of Leadership Development

At the Fourth Level of Influence, the "art" side of leadership is starting to outweigh the "science" side. However, this Fourth Level still embodies some very key steps.

Level 4 Leaders Compel Other Leaders to Get Team Results

At the previous Level of Influence, Level 3, the Leader was responsible for compelling people to *action*. The Level 4 Leader must compel people to obtain *results*. There is a big difference between getting people busy and making them effective. There is a time and place for activity as a focus, usually in the early days of a leader's experience. Activity breeds ability, confidence, and experience. But sooner or later, results are the name of the game. At Level 4, a leader's credibility comes from the results he is able to help *other* leaders attain.

Larry Bossidy, former CEO of Honeywell and former GE vice-chairman, has something he calls the Ultimate Metric. He said, "When you're confused about how you're doing as a leader, find out how the people you lead are doing. You'll know the answer." In *Attitudes and Altitudes*, author Pat Mesiti writes, "An effective leader is not someone who is loved or admired, but someone whose followers do the right things. Popularity is not leadership; results are. Mentoring is all about reproducing your values [and results] in others." A Level 4 Leader holds himself accountable for the results obtained in the lives of the people he leads and develops.

> *Activity breeds ability, confidence, and experience. But sooner or later, results are the name of the game.*

Level 4 Leaders Become Talent Scouts

Whenever an organization has effective Level 3 Leaders, it is a good bet that someone mentored and developed them. That is the job of a Level 4 Leader. Mike Shanahan, coach of the two-time Super Bowl Champion Denver Broncos and author of *Think Like a Champion*, tells us, "You can talk about teamwork, you can talk about sharing the load, you can talk about spreading it around all you want. But at some point, your leader has to emerge." Level 4 Leaders realize this and have the discretion to determine whom to spend time and energy developing. This requires the Level 4 Leader to recognize potential leadership talent. John Maxwell writes in *Equipping 101*, "Great leaders seek out and find potential leaders, then transform them into good leaders."

There are several qualities to look for when determining whom to mentor and develop into a leader. In *My Life and the Principles for Success* Ross Perot has a simpler list. He says, "Your success will be based on your judgment in building a great team of people. The people you want won't come to you—you have to search for them. Look for people who:

1. Are smart
2. Are tough
3. Are self-reliant
4. Have a record of achievement since childhood
5. Love to win."

Pastor Doug Murren said leaders come from the ranks of people who have the following:

1. The innovative urge
2. An above-average passion for principle
3. A need for affirmation that is much lower than average

4. A high level of curiosity
5. A track record of mastering failure.

Michael Abrashoff, former commander of the USS *Benfold* and author of *It's Your Ship*, said, "Bet on people who think for themselves," and added personal accountability as a must. Peter Schultz, former president of Porsche, said, "Hire attitude. Train skill." In *A Fish Out of Water* George Barna advises leaders to look for people who are:

1. Teachable
2. Have spiritual maturity
3. Perceive leadership to be an act of servant-hood
4. Have passion for the vision and for leading people toward it
5. Have sufficient basic skills that would enable them to add value to the team.

Jeff Immelt, CEO of General Electric, was quoted in Noel Tichy's book *The Cycle of Leadership* as saying he thinks that leaders at GE ought to start out with at least four key traits:

> First, you have got to be able to perform. There is nothing that replaces people who know how to perform in cycle after cycle; in good times and in bad. . . . Second, you want people who know how to learn every day. . . . Third, great people are going to have the ability to work in diverse global teams. . . . Fourth [is heart]. We have got to find a way to attract people who want to give back, give back to the environment, back to the community, give back to the workplace.

Pat Williams, senior vice-president of the Orlando Magic basketball team, said, "Psychological studies show that high-achieving, successful people are not overly concerned about what others think." Randy Haugen, successful Internet entrepreneur, tells us: "Great potential leaders:

1. Have a financial foundation
2. Have a relatability factor
3. Have credibility with their peers
4. Know a lot of people
5. Are confident
6. Are not worried what others think
7. Have personal discipline."

Notice how these lists have much in common. There is almost a "feeling" one gets about the makeup of correct leadership candidates when reading through them.

Recognizing potential leaders is not a black-and-white proposition, and these lists from giants in the leadership world are greatly appreciated. For the purpose of this book, the focus will be on a few key areas that have been found to be the most important when attempting to identify leaders worthy of mentoring and developing. This list starts with the three Foundational Qualities of Leadership with which we began:

1. Hungry
2. Hone-able
3. Honorable

These three are required, but when identifying potential leaders, there are a few more attributes to consider so that the Level 4 Leader does not waste time mentoring those who will not blossom into effective leaders. These are:

4. Activity
5. Respect

6. Connected relationship
7. Attitude
8. Relatability.

ACTIVITY

Activity is a highly important attribute to look for in those who can potentially be developed into leaders because this is a strong indicator of ambition, courage, and initiative. It also becomes a differentiator that the mentor can use to explain the privilege of becoming a protégé. The mentor, or Level 4 Leader, might say to the protégé, "The reason I have you here instead of a thousand other candidates is because you've convinced me through your efforts that you want to become a leader. If you will do what it takes and follow my counsel, I'll teach you what you need to succeed." When searching for potential leaders to develop, look for those with high levels of consistent activity, people who continually rotate through the Cycle of Achievement discussed earlier. It is impossible to steer a parked car, but a car in motion turns with ease. When it comes to finding potential leaders, look for someone in motion. Nearly everything else can be taught along the way.

During the American Civil War, President Abraham Lincoln suffered through a series of inept and ineffective generals at the head of the Union Army. The biggest challenge seemed to be finding someone who would take initiative and move the superior fighting force of the Union into battle against the ragtag Confederate Army. Some generals spent all their time drilling. Others spent their time in small, worthless skirmishes. Still others retreated just when the battle, and perhaps the war, would have been won. Time and again, Lincoln would remove a commander and replace him with another who promised to move the army into action. Finally, General Ulysses S. Grant

> "I can't spare this man; he fights."

proved to be the man. But as he took command of the Union forces and immediately moved into action, Grant was riddled with criticism. Lincoln's reply was an astute reminder of the importance of activity as the raw material of a leader. "I can't spare this man; he fights," said Lincoln.

Respect

Fundamental to the mentoring process is the concept of respect. If a candidate for leadership development does not respect the Level 4 Leader, his accomplishments, and his counsel, the process breaks down before it begins. There must be belief that the mentor can provide what the protégé needs to succeed as a leader. Michael Dell, founder of Dell Computer, writes in *Direct from Dell*, "For any company to succeed, it's critical for top management to share power successfully. You also need to respect one another, and communicate so constantly that you're practically of one mind on the most important topics and issues that face the company." That's what respect does: it breeds communication and cooperation and allows the successful sharing of power.

Connected Relationship

This term represents a relationship where the mentor and the protégé just seem to "connect." For teaching and learning, the most productive arrangement is a relationship where both sides genuinely like each other.

Attitude

It is impossible to teach leadership without continually returning to the topic of attitude. Winners don't have better circumstances; they have better attitudes about their circumstances. Herb Kelleher, CEO of highly profitable Southwest Airlines, says, "We'll train you on whatever it is you have to do, but the one thing Southwest cannot change in people is inherent attitudes."

Mentors should look closely for a positive attitude on the part of any candidate for leadership development. Without a proper attitude, there can be no personal growth.

RELATABILITY

Leaders are in the business of influencing *people*. For that reason, any candidate for the leadership-development process must have a basic ability with people. We call this "relatability." A relatable person is liked, trusted, and listened to. They make a good first impression and an even better impression as the relationship deepens. They exude credibility. Mentors looking for a potential leader to groom would be well advised to choose candidates who already have a high degree of this ability with people.

Level 4 Leaders Empower Other Leaders

At Level 4, leaders are not just developing *followers*, they are developing *leaders*. There is a big difference between the two.

Empowering leaders involves giving them control and decision-making authority. It means letting them lead their own teams and make their own mistakes and, quite simply, giving them the freedom to fail or fly. True leaders will not stick with the Level 4 Leader unless given a chance to spread their wings and show what they can do, because without that chance they will never reach their potential. This is why it is said that average leaders lead followers while great leaders lead leaders.

Level 4 Leaders Learn to Mentor

The next most important skill for a Level 4 Leader to develop is the ability to mentor. As writer H. Jackson Brown, Jr. said, "Talent without discipline is like an octopus on roller skates. There's plenty of movement, but you never know if it's going to be forward, backwards or sideways." Mentors harness the octopus.

> *Average leaders lead followers while great leaders lead leaders.*

The Level 3 Leader is a protégé to a mentor. At Level 4, he mentors others. Mentoring is an involved process that requires time, energy, discretion, patience, and discipline and it can be difficult to carry out. But there is really nothing that pays off as well for a leader as the ability to mentor other leaders to develop and grow. Here lies the secret to multiplication within an organization, and the secret to sustainable, continual growth of an organization's performance.

Mentoring and developing other leaders may seem like a lost art in today's "me first" society. We are aware that in many corporate positions "turf protection" rules the day. Many "leaders" are wary of developing others to become peak performers out of fear of losing their own cushy leadership positions. Allow us to give a caution: Leaders who become wrapped up in themselves and seek

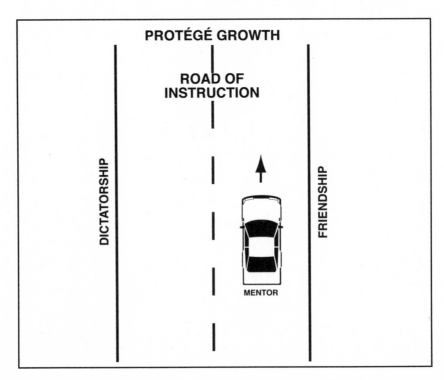

only their own success and aggrandizement rarely last for long in the field of leadership. True leaders are secure in their ability to perform and know that the only way to maximize themselves as leaders is to *develop other leaders*. There is a true win-win situation when a leader mentors and grows another leader. And without bringing others along, the leader has reached a plateau.

Level 4 Leaders must understand that the process of mentoring is a balancing act. Just as the road to success is bordered by Ditches of Discouragement and Complacency, the process of mentoring is bordered by the Ditches of Friendship and Dictatorship.

A mentor must stay just to the right of center. If a mentor becomes too much of a friend, the familiarity erodes respect and accountability that the protégé will have in the relationship. If a mentor drifts toward becoming a dictator, the protégé will feel resentful and hurt; he'll lose motivation and eventually respect for the mentor. A mentor is someone who cares about the performance of the protégé enough to say what a friend would not. In this regard, a mentor actually goes *beyond* friendship. But a mentor also respects the protégé too much ever to become bossy or demanding. There are statements mentors can use to make sure the protégé knows exactly where the relationship stands. One might be "Is it okay for me to rise above mere friendship and speak to you as a mentor?" This will remind the protégé that, although what is about to be said may not be easy to hear, it is for the good of the protégé. Alternately, a mentor might say, "I want to make sure you know that this is only what I recommend. You can do whatever you want. I am not your boss [if that be the case]. I only want what's best for you." With simple statements like these, the mentor can gently remind the protégé of the relationship and package the advice in its proper position.

> "Mentoring someone is not creating them in your own image, but giving them the opportunity to create themselves."

Mentors should never assume that each of their trainees should be treated in the same manner. People are different, and they require differing treatment. We don't mean to imply *unequal* treatment, but *unique* treatment. As famous film producer and director Steven Spielberg said, "Mentoring someone is not creating them in your own image, but giving them the opportunity to create themselves." This is done through understanding the protégé as a person and uncovering how he or she is "wired."

There are three main areas to identify when beginning to mentor someone. First is his or her personality or natural temperament. Since the ancient philosophers, there has been awareness that each of us arrives at birth with a basic personality temperament. It is beyond the scope of this book to delve into this in any detail, but leaders must know which of the temperaments are dominant in their protégés. Second, there are different learning styles. Some people learn best through visual instruction, others learn verbally, and still others learn best experientially. Third is the concept of "love languages." These are the styles of communication that a person prefers, such as verbal, touch, receiving gifts, quality time, and acts of service. Knowing these natural bents allows a mentor to provide spot-on instruction specifically tailored to the maximum impact on the individual being developed. This is not as complicated as it might first appear. Light reading on the topics of learning styles, love languages, and temperaments will familiarize you enough to understand and be able to identify how a given protégé is naturally inclined. This will facilitate the leadership-development process in tremendous ways.

Mentoring involves many steps. Much of it is more art than science. In fact, mentoring can be looked upon as long-term brain surgery. The overall intent is to teach the protégé how to think correctly as a leader. Ninety-five percent of mentoring is about helping the protégé develop proper thinking. In this section, we will break the process down into its component parts to reveal the art and teach the science.

SETS THE EXAMPLE

In *The Magic of Thinking Big*, David Schwartz writes, "Over a period of time, subordinates tend to become carbon copies of their chief. The simplest way to get high-level performance is to be sure the master-copy is worth duplicating." Example is an important part in all leadership functions, but especially in mentorship. Followers need help. Leaders need an example. So for a mentor to develop another leader, example is crucial. The protégé must have 100 percent confidence that the mentor knows of what he speaks. The proof is in the results. The mentor must have fruit on the tree to be an effective counselor, because to know and not to have is not to know. The only reason a protégé will listen to the mentor is because he believes the mentor can help him get what he wants.

ASKS QUESTIONS

With obvious results that command the respect of the protégé, the mentor can begin the counseling process. This begins by asking questions. The nature of these questions can vary, but they are driving at accomplishing a handful of specific objectives and geared toward a concept Stephen Covey, in *The Seven Habits of Highly Effective People*, calls "Seeking First to Understand." At first, the mentor simply has to get to know the protégé, because we cannot lead those we do not know. Regarding the protégé, the mentor wishes to know:

1. What makes him tick?
2. What makes him special?
3. Why did he get involved in his particular field?
4. What motivates him? What are his dreams?
5. What is his personality or temperament?

6. What challenges has he had in his life?
7. What victories has he had?
8. What principles does he understand and embody?
9. What principles does he still need to learn?
10. What blind spots does he have about himself?
11. What is his commitment level?
12. What is the basis of his character?
13. Where is his thinking?

The key for a mentor is to be a good listener. A mentor must learn to draw people out, to get them talking about themselves and their past experiences in ways that perhaps they rarely do. If the mentor gets someone talking long enough, he can learn nearly everything there is to know about him or her. It is as if the mentor is saying, "I want to get to know who you are so I can help you accomplish your dreams." A good mentor asks and listens and observes, taking mental notes, digging deeper into issues that are especially illuminating into the thinking of the protégé. Eventually, the mentor may be able to tell the protégé things about himself that even the protégé didn't know. Listening will tell the mentor where the protégé's thinking is and how he interprets information, what his perspective is, and how ambitious he really is for his goals.

BUILDS THE RELATIONSHIP

For the leadership-development process to be effective, the protégé must have 100 percent trust that what the mentor is telling him is in his best interest. Webster defines trust as the "assured reliance on the character, ability, strength, or truth of someone or something." This level of reliance can occur only where there is relationship. Mentors must seek to bond with their protégés, and there are no shortcuts when it comes to relationships. The mentor must invest time on a regular basis in building and se-

curing the relationship. This is especially important when it becomes
time for the mentor to provide course
correction or address issues of deficiency head-on. At that time, there

> *There are no shortcuts when it comes to relationships.*

had better be a relationship the mentor can draw upon. The old
saying still holds true: "People don't care how much you know
until they know how much you care." This is especially true for
the leadership-development process.

Author Stephen Covey provides an analogy that may be helpful in understanding the building of relationships. Picture the
goodwill in a relationship as a bank account. Both sides need time
and experiences together in order to deposit "goodwill" into each
other's accounts. Over time, the accounts grow and there is a surplus of goodwill. The more that accumulates, the higher the level
of trust between the two parties. Also, with a surplus balance built
up, there are sufficient "funds" of goodwill in case of a withdrawal.
In all relationships there will be those times when a comment
hurts feelings or one of the parties feels slighted or let down (i.e.,
a withdrawal). With sufficient funds in the bank account of goodwill, the relationship can survive the transaction and not become
bankrupt. "I'm sure Fred didn't mean anything by it" or "I'll for-
give her, because I know how she really feels about me" are the
natural responses in a relationship with surplus accounts. Leaders
understand this principle and make constant effort to put deposits
of goodwill into the accounts of their peers and subordinates on a
regular basis.

When a leader has a mentorship position, this concept becomes even more critical. This is because in the mentoring
process, it is often necessary—and indeed the very job of the mentor—to provide advice and counsel that is uncomfortable and
conceivably offensive to the protégé. If no account of goodwill has
been previously established, the relationship bankrupts and the

mentoring process fails. But with a solid relationship built on goodwill, the protégé takes the counsel and improves and grows. John Maxwell wrote, "Never underestimate the power of building relationships with people before asking them to follow you."

AFFIRMS THE PROTÉGÉ

Everyone needs to be accepted, and leaders are no different. Mentors affirm their protégés by accepting them where they are and approving of them as a person. This doesn't mean the mentor agrees with everything the growing leader does, but it does mean he accepts the protégé as a person of value and someone worthy of respect. The newer the relationship, the more important that the mentor remain nonjudgmental. There will be plenty of time throughout the leadership-development process to make adjustments and inspire personal growth. However, the doorway to positive change will never be opened unless the protégé is first accepted and affirmed for who he is at the outset.

BUILDS THE PROTÉGÉ'S BELIEF

It is very difficult to accomplish anything unless there is belief in the objective, the plan, the leadership, and the cause behind it all. On an even deeper level, it is very difficult to accomplish anything when a person doesn't have belief in his or her own ability. A mentor provides belief in all of these areas, but particularly in the self-belief category. This can be challenging. Even the strongest of leaders have self-doubts from time to time. Mentors stand by with evidences of past performance and reassurances from the well of their own experience to bolster the protégé's belief in himself and the possibility of achievement. Anthony Robbins explains that beliefs must be supported by upholding evidences, much as a stool must be upheld by its legs. The upholding legs of belief are comprised of:

1. evidence of past performance
2. character
3. values

Mentors help bolster the belief a protégé has in herself by reminding her of these supporting evidences. Having someone who believes in her and, more importantly, who helps her believe in herself is a critical component to high achievement. Effective Level 4 Leaders fulfill that responsibility.

Builds the Protégé's Dream

Another key component of a mentor's responsibilities is to help the protégé develop his dream. Mentors have walked and seen farther, and they can help the protégé dream and think bigger than he could on his own. Many times leaders cannot see how far their own greatness will carry them, but a mentor can. As John Wanamaker observes, "A man is not doing much until the cause he works for possesses all there is of him."

Kills the Protégé's Fear

Fear is the show-stopper that arrests the development of a leader at the edge of his comfort zone. Mentors provide the jail break. This can be done through reframing situations to help protégés see things in a different light. It may be done by exposing the issues causing anxiety for the wafer-thin obstacles they really are. Usually, it involves the mentor encouraging the protégé to confront his fears head-on. As the saying goes, "Ninety-five percent of the things we worry about will never happen, and the 5 percent that do are not as bad as we had thought." When leaders perform and push through their comfort zones, they are often amazed at the minuscule resistance they encountered compared to what they had feared. Just pushing through these barriers is a fear-killer, and mentors are there to provide that push with courage on loan.

Courage is not action without fear but action in spite of fear. Mentors foster that courage.

GIVES CONFIDENCE

One way mentors engender courage in the hearts of their protégés is by building their confidence. It has been said that confidence is a fragile thing. One minute a leader is soaring and the next crashing. Mentors help build and restore confidence by pointing out past victories and reminding the leader of his strengths and abilities. "This is not a big deal," says the mentor, "you've been here before. With your strengths, you can handle this one, too." A mentor builds confidence by being specific. Flattery and loose words mean nothing, and may actually serve to diminish a leader's confidence even further. A mentor knows the abilities and past successes of his student and mentions them specifically. "Remember that time you overcame X problem? How did you do that? Well, you'll do this the same way, and you're a much stronger leader than you were then." This type of reinforcement builds confidence and allows the leader to maximize instead of being paralyzed by doubt and fear.

KEEPS THE PROTÉGÉ IN THE ACTION PHASE

Another way mentors build confidence is by keeping their protégés in the game. Confidence in performance usually slackens when the leader's activity level drops. Remembering past victories and performances goes only so far. There is nothing like new success to bolster confidence, and mentors take advantage of this truth. Keeping their protégés in the game is half the battle of building confidence.

The action phase is also required for the development of proper habits. If leaders can get their people to do enough of the correct things on a regular basis, eventually those things will become habits. When leaders develop good habits, their capability becomes an unconscious competence; they can perform well without having to stop and think too much about it. Repeated performance of the right things over time will build a proper set of instincts. For a leader, developing good instincts becomes a must. Often a leader has little time to make key decisions. The ability to make correct decisions in the heat of battle can be developed only by living in the action phase long enough to gain effective habits and have good judgment become part of one's instincts. None of this can be learned anywhere else except in the action phase. Good mentors keep their protégés highly engaged in the action phase to foster this development.

> *It's not what happens, but how the leader sees what happens, that counts.*

REFRAMES THE PROTÉGÉ'S CHALLENGES

Mentors must have the ability to see things in their proper light and then help shed that light into the mind of the protégé. It may happen occasionally that leaders are too close to the forest to see the trees. Sometimes a soldier in battle has no perspective on whether his side is winning the war. Mentors can provide perspective on the challenges facing a leader. This is done through reframing, where the mentor takes the challenge as defined by the protégé and "reframes" it in a different light. The protégé may see only lemons, but the mentor shows how to make them into lemonade. The protégé may see only the clouds, but the mentor sees the silver lining. This is a very important skill and goes straight to the heart of the task of a mentor. Reframing problems and challenges allows the protégé a window into a solution. It is nothing more than presenting the evidence in a way that convinces the leader that he can still have success. Without proper reframing, obstacles can look insurmountable. "It may look like that to you now," says the mentor, "but I assure you, when it happened to me, it turned out to be the very opposite. Look at it this way." It's not what happens, but how the leader sees what happens, that counts. Mentors help their leaders see things in the proper way.

ALLOWS STRUGGLE TO INSTRUCT

Every mentor knows that the struggles his protégé will encounter are there to instruct. While it is important to reframe challenges and obstacles in the proper perspective as we have just discussed, it is also the job of the mentor to allow struggles to impart their wisdom. It is rightly said that we learn more from our mistakes than any of our successes. American novelist Herman Melville said, "He who has never failed somewhere, that man can not be great." In the case of any great leader it was the struggles that made him great. In *Know Your Limits—Then Ignore Them*, John Mason states, "Problems are the price of progress. The obstacles of life are intended to make us better, not bitter."

> **"Problems are the price of progress."**

There is a concept called a "desert experience." Moses was forced to march the Israelites through the desert for forty years to condition them as a people to inherit the promised land of Canaan. Jesus went out into the desert to pray and prove his ability to resist temptation totally. President Ronald Reagan is said to have encountered his "desert experience" when his movie-star career and marriage ended almost simultaneously following World War II. He had been a rising star actor making hundreds of movies and was married to the Actress of the Year, but a divorce and a change in his contracts left him alone, doing small bit-parts on television and traveling the country as a national spokesperson for General Electric. It was a drop in status few people would relish, and it lasted for years.

But one of Reagan's biographers, Peggy Noonan, tells of how the years on the road speaking for General Electric actually *built*

Ronald Reagan the politician. He was able to speak rather freely on the political subjects he cared about most while honing his communication abilities. (It was no accident that he later became known even by his critics as "the Great Communicator.") Additionally, he circulated from town to town meeting tens of thousands of people and learning about "mainstream America" and how it thought. It was the skills he learned in those lean years, his desert experience, that armed him for what was to be one of the greatest presidencies in United States history. It is said that every problem introduces a man to himself, and Reagan's speechmaking years introduced the actor to the statesman.

Level 4 Leaders know that their protégés will be honed in the fiery furnace of struggle, and they allow it and help impart the lessons being learned along the way. As mentors, Level 4 leaders must help their protégés realize that

> **Every leader needs encouragement.**

the breakfast of champions is not cereal, but struggle. After all, struggle is the seasoning that makes victory taste sweet.

ENCOURAGES THE PROTÉGÉ

On the heels of reframing comes encouragement. Every leader needs encouragement. Mentors let protégés know that they have the seeds of greatness deep inside, that they *do* have what it takes to make it.

When Nathaniel Hawthorne, a heartbroken man, went home to tell his wife that he had been fired from his job in a customhouse and confessed that he was a failure, she surprised him with an exclamation of joy.

She said triumphantly, "Now you can write your book!"

He replied with sagging confidence, "Yes, and what shall we live on while I am writing it?"

To his amazement, she opened a drawer and pulled out a substantial amount of money.

He exclaimed, "Where on earth did you get that?"

She answered, "I have always known that you were a man of genius. I knew that someday you would write a masterpiece. So every week out of the money you have given me for housekeeping, I have saved something; here is enough to last us for one whole year."

> "The real secret of success is enthusiasm."

From her trust and confidence came one of the greatest novels of American literature: *The Scarlet Letter*. Sometimes encouragement is all that's needed.

SPREADS CONTAGIOUS ENTHUSIASM

Ralph Waldo Emerson said, "Nothing great was ever achieved without enthusiasm." Walter Chrysler tells us, "The real secret of success is enthusiasm. Yes, more than enthusiasm I would say excitement. I like to see men get excited. When they get excited, they make a success of their lives." These qualities of enthusiasm and excitement must be demonstrated by mentors. Enthusiasm is contagious, like a fire in dry wood, spreading from place to place. Mentors are first starters and fire stokers, keeping the flames of excitement in their protégés burning bright. Enthusiasm is a feeling, and mentors must become adept at transferring that feeling.

When Vince Lombardi took over as the head coach of the Green Bay Packers, they had bottomed out. Their record the previous year was ten losses and one tie out of twelve games. According to an article in *Guideposts* magazine, Lombardi showed up and said, "Gentlemen, we are going to have a football team. We are going to win some games. Get that! You are going to learn how to block, run and tackle. You are going to outplay all the teams that come up against you. You are to have confidence in me and enthusiasm for my system. Hereafter, I want you to think of only three things: your home, your religion, and the Green Bay Packers! Let enthusiasm take a hold of you!" From there, the Green Bay Packers went on to be the most dominant team for a decade. Vince Lombardi, the mentor, had not only transferred a feeling of enthusiasm, he had demanded it! And he demanded that his players be enthusiastic not only about him as their coach, but also about his system as well! Level 4 Leaders know how to generate that type of enthusiasm in their leaders.

TEACHES THE PHILOSOPHY

All effective organizations and their leaders have a philosophy of success, a road map of behavior and thinking that explains and continues their history of accomplishment. It is the job of a Level 4 Leader to inculcate that philosophy into the hearts and minds of the leaders being developed. Every interaction between the mentor and his protégé is an opportunity to preach and teach the winning philosophy.

Bill Walsh, former head coach of the San Francisco 49ers, said of John Wooden, the most successful coach in all of sports history, "John Wooden is a 'philosopher-coach' in the truest sense: a man whose beliefs, teachings, and wisdom go far beyond sports, and ultimately address how to bring out the very best in yourself and others in all areas of life. He is a master teacher who understands motivation, organization, and psychology. Coach Wooden is able to successfully share his wisdom because he has a gift for expressing his philosophy directly and simply, in a manner accessible and applicable to everyone." The ability to express and share a winning philosophy is a core competency for any mentor. If it worked for the most successful athletic coach in history, it is worthy of modeling by mentors in every field.

> *To have a high quality of life, we must have a high quality of thought.*

Imparts his Thinking (Common Sense)

The most important gift any successful leader has to share with others is his way of thinking. To have a high quality of life, we must have a high quality of thought. Author David Schwartz, in *The Magic of Thinking Big*, says, "Where success is concerned, people are not measured in inches, or pounds, or college degrees, or family background; they are measured by the size of their thinking. How big we think determines the size of our accomplishments. Remember, the main job of the leader is thinking. And the best preparation for leadership is thinking." It follows that one of the most important objectives for a mentor is gradually to impart his entire way of thinking into the protégé. This is not an easy or a fast process. It can result only as a product of time spent together addressing issues in a constructive way. It requires diligent study on the part of the protégé and careful questioning and instruction from the mentor. As time goes on, the protégé should react to new circumstances with a question: What would my mentor think about this? Eventually, in a well-developed relationship, the protégé will take challenges to the mentor with a best-guess analysis of what the mentor will most likely say and recommend. In this way, the protégé can embody the thinking and learn to apply it to whatever comes along.

Course-Corrects and Confronts the Issues

We discussed this concept of course correction in the Cycle of Achievement when we stressed the importance of seeking counsel. This is a very big area of operation for a Level 4 Leader. When mentoring, it's a leader's job to identify where the protégé is off track and provide correction to get him back on track.

1. What principles is the protégé missing?
2. What are his thinking patterns and how are they wrong?
3. How is his perspective in need of reframing?

4. How can the protégé see things differently so that he behaves or performs more effectively?
5. How are his attitudes inappropriate or unproductive?
6. What does the protégé need to see that he doesn't see and how can the mentor help him see it?

These are the types of questions a mentor explores when listening to the protégé and probing for a correct view of the situation. It is here that listening and knowing the protégé are absolute prerequisites. In effect, a mentor helps the protégé see himself. This is necessary because all of us have "blind spots" in our lives. These are

> *In effect, a mentor helps the protégé see himself.*

problems or weaknesses that we just cannot see ourselves (though others may). Mentors will notice that their protégés are both "willfully blind" and "blindly willful" when it comes to these blind spots, and it is the mentor's job to help the protégé confront these areas.

It is as if the mentor holds up a mirror of truth so the student can put away his mirror of self-deception.

Course correction must be done in love. Remember, the protégé must first know beyond doubt that the mentor has his best interests at heart. He must know that the mentor would never intentionally say anything to hurt him. Only upon this platform can effective course correction be provided. The terminology we like comes from Josh McDowell and Bob Hostetler in their excellent book, *The New Tolerance*. McDowell and Hostetler say that we must speak with "humble truth and aggressive love." Humble truth says that course correction occurs gently and in kindness so that the protégé does not become demoralized. Aggressive love says that the feeling of care and respect is so strong that the mentor is free to administer correction without hurting the feelings or pride of the protégé.

How many of us are more instinctively inclined to do the opposite and speak instead with aggressive truth and humble love? Paul David Tripp, author of *Instruments in the Redeemer's Hands*, writes, "We don't want to serve others in a way that requires . . . personal sacrifice. We would prefer to lob grenades of truth into people's lives rather than lay down our lives for them." Level 4 Leaders must never simply "lob grenades of truth" at their people; they must first take the time to establish aggressive love. As author Stevenson Willis wrote, "Tact is the velvet hammer which softens the blows of truth that is hard." Ravi Zacharias says, "If we have taken off someone's nose, what good does it do for us to then hand them a rose?" Level 4 Leaders know that the stronger the love the stronger the allowable correction.

> *"If we have taken off someone's nose, what good does it do for us to then hand them a rose?"*

There is a saying that true conclusions cannot come from faulty assumptions. Mentors help protégés confront issues that are holding them back by assessing assumptions head-on.

The degree to which the mentor and protégé share mutual respect can be measured by the amount of honesty that exists between them. And honesty will be required to confront issues and clear obstacles effectively.

In the area of personal growth, the operative fundamental is that the lesson continues until the lesson is learned. If an organization doesn't move forward, it is because the leader is not addressing the issues in his or her path. Mentors can help point out these issues and compel the leader to make changes that will get things moving forward again.

Picture the progress of an organization as a tide of rushing water. It is the leader's job to clear all obstacles out of the path of the rushing water. When the flow rushes up against a blockage, the flow stops and the leader is needed to remove the obstacle. If he doesn't, the organization sits in waiting, making no progress. Sometimes the issue is with the leader himself; he may be blocking the water. Mentors help the leader identify these issues and remove blockages and/or get out of the way. There will be times when the issues to be confronted are not comfortable or pleasant but need to be addressed regardless. It is at such times that mentors and leaders both must muster the courage to do what is necessary.

> *Mentors must learn to use "velvet sledge hammers" when removing flies from the foreheads of their protégés.*

This process of confronting issues requires close observance and listening, but it also demands tact, as we said above. Mentors must learn to use "velvet sledge hammers" when removing flies from the foreheads of their protégés. Issues must be addressed, and the best method is to attack them when issues are still small. Recall that it's easier to pluck out a tiny twig now than cut down a large oak later.

One of the best techniques for addressing areas of concern with protégés is the "sandwich method." This involves complimenting the student leader on areas of strength and on specific noteworthy accomplishments. Next, the mentor addresses the problem with warmth and understanding, but nonetheless boldly. It should be the object of the mentor to "get it all out on the table." Finally, once the issues have been directly confronted and discussed to their productive conclusion (protégé acknowledgment, commitment to improve or correct the issue, all questions answered), the mentor can then exit the discussion by building up the trainee again, reminding the trainee about his or her opportunities and emphasizing that it has been the behavior and not the person that has been corrected. Remember, it is vital that the protégé understand how much the mentor cares. It would certainly be easier for the mentor to ignore uncomfortable conversations (at least in the moment), but the mentor addresses these things because he or she cares about the student.

GETS THE PROTÉGÉ TO TAKE RESPONSIBILITY

A very large part of mentoring involves the concept of taking responsibility. It is a natural tendency for each of us to search for excuses or alibis when things don't go our way. Leaders do not have this luxury. Mentors must train their protégés in the art of taking responsibility not only for their actions, but also for their results.

> *Mentors must train their protégés in the art of taking responsibility not only for their actions, but also for their results.*

In 1899 a small article written by a man named Elbert Hubbard appeared in the magazine *The Philistine*. It told the story of a meeting between the president of the United States, William McKinley, and Colonel Arthur Wagner, head of the Bureau of Military Intelligence for the United States. The war with Spain on the island of Cuba was coming to a boil, and the United States was in desperate need of communicating with the Cuban insurgent leader General Calixto Garcia. General Garcia was known only to be in the mountains of Cuba leading rebel troops in their fight for freedom. His exact whereabouts were unknown.

Colonel Wagner told the president, "I have a man—a young officer, Lieutenant Andrew Summers Rowan. If anybody can get a message to Garcia, Rowan can." Colonel Wagner then instructed Lieutenant Rowan, "You must carry a message to General Garcia, who will be found somewhere in the eastern part of Cuba. . . . You must plan and act for yourself. The task is yours and yours only. Get that message to Garcia." Three weeks after receiving his orders, Lieutenant Rowan returned to Washington with the news that he had successfully delivered the message, and opened the lines of communication.

In the words of Elbert Hubbard, "The point I wish to make is this: McKinley gave Rowan a letter to be delivered to Garcia. Rowan took the letter and did not ask, 'Where is he at?' By the eternal, there is a man whose form should be cast in deathless bronze and the statue placed in every college of the land. It is not book learning young men need, nor instruction about this and that, but a stiffening of the vertebrae which will cause them to be loyal to a trust, to act promptly, concentrate their energies: do the thing, 'Carry a message to Garcia.'

"And the man, who, when given a letter for Garcia, quietly takes the missive, without asking any idiotic questions, and with no lurking intention of chucking it into the nearest sewer, or of doing anything else but deliver it, never gets laid off, nor has to go on a strike for higher wages. Civilization is one long anxious search for just such individuals. Anything such a man asks shall be granted. His kind is so rare that no employer can afford to let him go. He is wanted in every city, town, and village; in every office, shop, store and factory. The world cries out for such. He is needed and needed badly, the man who can carry a message to Garcia." Lieutenant Rowan took responsibility, period. That's what leadership is all about, and that is what Level 4 Leaders must get the leaders they are developing to understand and embody.

> *The attitude of a mentor should be "I won't take the credit when you win. I won't take the blame when you don't."*

The attitude of a mentor should be "I won't take the credit when you win. I won't take the blame when you don't." Earlier, when we talked about accepting the blame and sharing the credit, we were discussing a leader's general position at the helm of a team. In the mentoring process, however, the mentor passes the accountability to the protégé. It is as if the baton of leadership is being passed. Now it is the protégé's war, and the mentor is teaching him to lead it.

Remember, the mentor already has fruit on the tree to demonstrate that his information has value. The protégé must then take that information and assume responsibility for its implementation, and the results of that implementation.

HOLDS THE PROTÉGÉ ACCOUNTABLE

Leaders are accountable for their own actions, period. It is the job of the mentor to teach this habit. It begins when the mentor holds the developing leader accountable for his results, and "forces" him to measure up to his true potential. This works because people will often do for the approval of someone else what they won't accomplish for themselves. A relationship is cultivated in which the protégé wants to perform to earn the respect of the

> *"There is nothing greater than a challenge."*

mentor. In fact, earning respect is a prerequisite to continuing the training. If a mentor is giving time and energy to the development of a future leader and nothing is changing or improving (measurable improvement in a reasonable amount of time), then the mentor is wasting time and should find a more worthy student.

Pat Summitt, author of *Reach for the Summit*, said of her role as a basketball coach, "I only promise what I can deliver. I don't guarantee success. I tell our players, 'If you work with me, I'll help you be the player you *should* be.' I'll get them to that point, but *they* have to take those final steps."

CHALLENGES THE PROTÉGÉ

Hunger and *desire* are key to the ongoing development of a protégé. This springs largely from the challenge a leader feels to perform; and for high achievers, the greater the challenge, the greater the performance. When Michael Jordan retired the first time from basketball and decided to play baseball instead, it was because he felt he had run out of challenges on the basketball court. Terry Bradshaw, four-time Super Bowl winning quarterback of the Pittsburgh Steelers, says, "There is nothing greater than a challenge."

Mentors make sure their developing leaders remain challenged. Questions a Level 4 Leader or mentor might ask to be sure the protégé is challenged are:

1. What vision are you currently pursuing?
2. What goals do you have to fulfill that vision?
3. What type of activity would be required to accomplish that?
4. Are you willing to do the work?
5. How strong is your commitment?
6. What type of person would be required to accomplish that?
7. Are you willing to change to become that person?

Keeping leaders challenged fuels their growth and gives them the power to improve their way upward through increasing Levels of Influence.

Pursues a Heart Change

All these steps in mentoring are fine, but they will add up to nothing if they somehow bypass the heart. In *Intruments in the Redeemer's Hands* Paul David Tripp writes, "If the heart doesn't change, the person's words and behavior may change temporarily because of an external pressure or incentive. But when the pressure or incentive is removed, the changes will disappear. The body always goes where the heart leads." Tripp then goes on to give an illuminating example, which we'll paraphrase below.

Suppose there were an apple tree that grew substandard fruit year after year, with dry, miscolored produce. Tired of not getting good-tasting, healthy fruit from the tree, a gardener takes branch cutters, a staple gun, and some colored construction paper out to the base of the tree. Climbing a ladder, the gardener cuts each piece of poor fruit from the tree and staples a paper rendition of a perfectly ripe apple to each branch instead. This example is obviously ludicrous, because merely giving the appearance of healthy fruit does nothing to produce a better harvest. Likewise, anytime we address human issues by dressing up the subject with outward appearances of change, we are equally ludicrous because we miss the root of the issues at hand.

> *"Change that ignores the heart will seldom transform the life."*

Summarizes Tripp: "There is an undeniable root and fruit connection between our heart and our behavior. People and situations do not determine our behavior; they provide the occasion where our behavior reveals our hearts. Lasting change always takes place through the pathway of the heart. Therefore, the heart is our target in personal growth and ministry."

Tripp's words go to the heart of the matter (pun intended). Mentors must target the hearts of their protégés if there is to be lasting change, true growth, and harvestable fruit. Too many times people make changes on the outside but become discouraged when the results don't last. That is because they have not committed to change way down deep, at the level of the heart. Mentors pursue change and growth in the heart of their protégés because that is the only place where change lasts. The results come later and are obvious and sustained.

Develops Balance in the Protégé

It may be helpful at this point to share the five categories or areas of personal growth that may be used throughout the course of developing a leader. These categories are:

1. Finances
2. Faith
3. Family
4. Friends
5. Fitness

These five areas can be compared to the spokes of a wagon wheel. Any spoke out of balance with the others drastically affects the operation of the wheel. In the life of a protégé, the same holds true. A person's wellness in one area affects the others. It only stands to reason that growth in all the categories helps in the life of the protégé across the board. Conversely, poor performance in one or two areas will affect the other categories in a negative sense. And for some reason, the negative seems to be many times more capable of spreading across the categories than the positive. Over time, one of the objects of the leadership-development process is to enhance each of the categories and eventually arrive at a balance or harmony among them.

Finances are first. This is because the mentoring process usually starts in a career setting, which has a direct impact on finances. But the disciplines that are required not only to earn more money, but to save, budget, and invest, are extremely valuable to building confidence and stability. Finances are also very measurable, and underscore the ability of the mentor to help the protégé succeed.

Faith is really the most important. After all, submitting to God and fulfilling His purpose in life is ultimately what life is all about. Further, strong faith in a calling and purpose are essential for significance as a leader. However, it may take a while before a protégé feels comfortable enough with a mentor to open up in this area. Nonetheless, this area must be addressed as a major focal point for ongoing growth.

Family is critical, also. It really doesn't matter how successful a leader becomes if he doesn't have his private life put together. Strife at home in the most personal, private relationships we have is poison to our well-being, happiness, and

> *It really doesn't matter how successful a leader becomes if he doesn't have his private life put together.*

productivity. Mentors will not omit this area if they truly want to help developing leaders achieve complete success.

Friends are a crucial consideration in the growth of a leader. This is because for so many people, the crowd they associate with is not productive in their life. Many times people who strongly desire to change and grow, who even begin making some of the tough decisions and steps in that direction, continue associating with their old friends and acquaintances. At worst, these associations are destructive to their personal growth and often blow them from the path of success altogether. At best, these relationships add little value.

Two sayings apply here. "We are who we hang around," and "If we want to change some things in our life, we've got to change some things in our life!" For most, this begins with the people to whom they give the hours of their life. Mentors know upcoming leaders must choose their association with others wisely.

Fitness makes the list, of course, because none of the successes or responsibilities of a leader mean anything if the leader is in poor health. Not only do proper diet and exercise help the leader live longer to enjoy the fruits of his labor and maximize his contributions to the world, but they also make him more energized and effective in his daily living.

It is understandable that keeping the five spokes of the wheel exactly in balance is unrealistic, but as Vince Lombardi said, "We are going to give perfection one [heck] of a chase, and if we never get it, we'll certainly catch excellence along the way!" Spoken like a true mentor!

Developing Leaders: Lord Horatio Nelson
"A Band of Brothers"

After only one year as an admiral and still yet only thirty-nine years old, an Englishman demonstrated the rare ability not only to lead, but to develop other leaders as well. When the moment of truth arrived, this ability proved critical, tilting the balance of world power and ensuring the future of free societies.

It was summer 1798. A young upstart named Napoleon Bonaparte was rapidly ascending to power in the French army. In April of that year, Bonaparte became commander in chief of the Army of the East and was ordered to take possession of Egypt in the name of the Republic of France.

Bold, brash, and brave, Bonaparte was well suited for the task. Long an admirer of Eastern culture, he dreamed of establishing an Eastern Empire rich in scholarship and art, with himself, of course, in the seat of power. Napoleon's secret plan was to sail his large force the length of the Mediterranean and first attack Egypt, then move through Syria and Persia to India.

France's staunch enemy, England, knew of the enormous expeditionary force that was being formed but could not determine its target or route. Further, the English lived in constant fear of French invasion on their isolated island, and were required to keep much of the strength of their army and navy at home for defense. The best hope of defeating Napoleon would be on the open water, before he could disembark his powerful army upon some unknown shore. Politically, this would serve to bring many of the other countries of Europe and Asia into an alliance against the aggressive French. Although without knowing where Napoleon was headed, it would be a near miracle to find him once he had set sail upon the enormous Mediterranean Sea. In addition, the number of ships it would take, spread out as a net, to find Napoleon's force just simply didn't exist. The best chance would be to intercept the expedition as it left France. This would most likely occur at the port of Toulon, one of southern France's main naval ports and the one most likely to accommodate such a massive campaign.

Command of the English naval squadron sent to intercept and destroy Napoleon's force was given to a man named Horatio

Nelson, recently recovered from the loss of his right arm at the attack on Santa Cruz de Tenerife, and previously blinded in one eye from the siege of Calvi in 1794. When introduced to King George the king proclaimed, "You have lost your right arm! Your country has a claim for a bit more of you." And indeed it did.

What followed was one of the most famous episodes of "cat and mouse" in military history. A massive storm damaged Nelson's ship and several others in his fleet, and gave the French just enough time to escape the waters of Toulon. Further, the storm separated Nelson from a rendezvous with his "frigates," which, much like cavalry in those days, served as the "eyes and ears" of a fleet. Frigates were fast and light and could sail quickly across large areas of open ocean, spot enemy squadrons, and race back to the main fleet to alert them where to find the enemy to attack. Separated from them, Nelson was without the best form of reconnaissance available, and was left to search for Napoleon as if groping in the dark. But there was good news. The scheduled reinforcement from England arrived in the form of a fifty-gun ship and ten seventy-gun ships. With this sizeable fleet and its many young and able captains, Nelson began the hunt.

According to Nathan Miller in *Broadsides*, "An encounter between history's greatest general and greatest admiral seemed imminent." It was more than that. France had become the world's preeminent military power. England had become the world's dominant navy. In what would be branded the War between the Whale and Elephant, old concepts of power would be clashing with new, and Dictatorship would be squaring off against Democracy.

Napoleon rendezvoused with more divisions in Corsica and then sailed to attack Malta, secure in the rumor that Nelson's ship had foundered at Sardinia and put in for repairs. Nelson, in the meantime, had received information that convinced him Napoleon was sailing to attack Naples, so he charged his fleet in that direction. A little later Nelson learned of the attack on Malta, and crowded on as much sail as possible to arrive at that island quickly. Before reaching Malta, however, Nelson received word that the French had already conquered it (true) and had sailed onward (false). Convinced correctly now that Napoleon's ultimate target was the city of Alexandria in Egypt, Nelson changed course and sped directly there.

Somehow, the British fleet unknowingly passed by the French fleet, which had finally departed Malta. It had been a very misty night and the French had heard the British signal guns ringing out through the night air, so they hushed all activity. Unbeknownst to them, the British fleet sailed by and beat the French to Alexandria by days. Upon arriving, the British investigated and found no sign of the French. Without his frigates to scout around and verify anything, Nelson was forced to hunt on, moving farther eastward in the Mediterranean. Still there was no sign of the French. Thinking that perhaps Naples had been Napoleon's target after all, Nelson turned his fleet around and sailed westward yet again, leaving Egypt open to the devastating French attack that would come just days later. History records that the French reached Alexandria on the very day the topgallant masts of Nelson's fleet were disappearing over the horizon. Nelson made it all the way to Naples again before receiving the news that the French fleet had indeed landed at Alexandria. He once again turned around and sailed back in hot pursuit.

It was during the days and nights of this heralding chase that Nelson intensified the development of the young captains of the ships under his command. According to Miller:

> Throughout the voyage, whenever the weather permitted, he invited groups of his captains to [his flagship's] great cabin, where, over dinner, as Captain Berry related, "he would fully develop to them his own ideas of the different and best modes of

attack, and such plans as he proposed to execute upon falling in with the enemy, whatever their position might be, by day or night." In this "school for captains" they came to know Nelson's intentions so well, Berry added, that in battle, signals were nearly unnecessary. Soon they became, in Nelson's words, "a Band of Brothers."

Nelson finally found the French fleet anchored near Alexandria in Aboukir Bay: thirteen ships of the line, four large frigates, and a host of other smaller vessels. The French were prepared for an invasion, though, and had arranged their ships in a very effective defensive posture along a line of shoals and dangerous rocks. The battle ships were placed on the outer, protective line, while the smaller vessels were all tucked safely behind. Further, the French ships had springs attached to their anchor lines, which would allow them to be easily maneuvered into various firing angles. Cannon filled the nearby shore and had been prepared to increase the French fleet's defensive firepower, having taken the weapons from the landward side of the ships that wouldn't otherwise be useful against an attack. Additionally, the French fleet contained more overall firepower than that of the British: 1,026 guns to only 740. Such a well-placed, armed, and anchored line of ships was usually invincible. The final obstacle, normally deadly to sea battles and especially those close to shore, was that it was nearly nightfall!

Once the battle had commenced, Nelson was forced to rely on the performances of his captains. It was too dark, too loud, and too confusing to use signal flutes or flags for communication. According to Colin White, author of multiple books about Nelson, "It was one of the most ferocious and decisive naval battles of the sailing era. Nelson's battle plans had been agreed with his captains some time before. As a result, having made his decision to attack at once, even though night was falling, he was able to leave the detailed conduct of the action to his subordinates." Nathan Miller writes, "On innumerable occasions, he [Nelson] had discussed his plans with his captains for dealing with the French if he found them at anchor. There was no time for consultation or elaborate signals—and there was no need for them. Every captain knew what was in the admiral's mind."

This proved monumental. At the start of the attack, one of Nelson's commanders saw an opening between two of the French ships and sailed right through it, using an almost unheard-of battle technique, breaking with all the customs of the past, and giving him the opportunity to sail along the landward side of the French fleet's defensive line. Another captain took a similar initiative at a different place in the line, and soon the entire French fleet was engulfed by gunfire from both sides, unable to return the fire from the landward side because of their offloaded cannon, which had been taken ashore. Those shore cannon were somehow just out of range of the attacking English ships and therefore helpless to engage in the battle.

"Friendly fire," that sad condition occurring when an army accidentally fires upon its own members, was one of night fighting's greatest dangers, and especially when ships were firing upon both sides of an enemy vessel. However, Nelson's training of his captains came to the rescue here as well. In the many preparatory talks Nelson had given his captains, they had prearranged to suspend four lanterns from a certain location on each ship to make them easily identifiable in the darkness. Of the immense and vicious battle that was to ensue, Nelson said of his captains, "Each knew his duty."

Nelson himself received a nasty head wound and thought himself mortally wounded. He was rushed belowdecks to the surgeon but refused to cut in line ahead of his many wounded sailors. "I will take my turn with my brave fellows," he said. As morning came, after twelve hours of non-stop thunderous fighting, many of those brave fellows were collapsed asleep on their cannon.

Miller concluded:

> No other victory of the Age of Fighting Sail was so astonishingly complete. . . . Of the thirteen French ships of the line that had cleared for action the day before, nine had been captured, two had burned, and only two escaped. The French lost 1,700 men killed, 1,500 wounded, and 3,000 taken prisoner. British casualties totaled 218 killed and 677 wounded, including the admiral himself. All of the elements of what would become known as the "Nelson Touch" were clearly visible at the Battle of the Nile: inspiring leadership, the intensive training of his captains, the delegation of crucial tactical decisions to them in the heat of battle rather than slavish adherence to [common practices], and the taking of calculated risks to ensure that a battle would be not only decisive but devastating to an enemy fleet.

Nelson would write of his triumph that day, "Victory is not a name strong enough for such a scene." As put by author Alan Schom in *Napoleon Bonaparte*, "One month after their arrival, Napoleon and his army were—to all intents and purposes—virtual prisoners in Egypt." Napoleon and his Grand Army of the East were stranded.

Additionally, Nelson's victory emboldened the governments of Turkey, Russia, Austria, and Naples, who all joined the British in a coalition against France. Napoleon would rise to crown himself emperor of France and rule much of continental Europe, but his dominion would be limited and ultimately fail, at least in part, because of his first defeat suffered at the hands of the British navy. From that, he would never fully recover.

Nelson and his captains had done it. Such an enormous, one-sided victory could not have been obtained by one man. Nor could it have been accomplished by leadership practices of a lower level than that employed. (*Without developing other leaders, one is limited to the performance of only followers.*) The victory required the coordinated effort of *many leaders*. Although the British government had received tremendous criticism for entrusting the operation to so young a commander, Nelson had demonstrated his ability not only as a seaman, but also as a *leader of other leaders*. Napoleon himself would later say, "If it had not been for you English, I should have been emperor of the East; but wherever there is water to float a ship, we are to find you in our way." This was due in large part to the legacy begun by Nelson and his captains, which continued through the remainder of the century. (*Level 4 Leaders leave a legacy through the leaders they develop.*)

Nelson was a true Level 4 Leader. He had *found and developed other leaders* capable of performing at the levels he himself had earlier in his illustrious career, thereby significantly expanding his influence. (*A Level 4 Leader is only as good as the leaders he develops.*) The men admired Nelson for his remarkable war record, and not only bought in to him as their leader, but also bought in to the vision of annihilating the French fleet and crushing Napoleon. (*Leaders must buy in to their leader and the vision.*) He took them under his wing, giving careful instruction, teaching them his fighting philosophy and his way of thinking, and empowering them with the responsibility for results when it mattered most (*empowering other leaders to lead their own teams, giving them the freedom to succeed as leaders in their own right*). As they succeeded, he worked for their promotion and advancement, writing flowery letters of praise for the newspapers and their naval superiors (*publicly praised and recognized correct behavior*). Even when he was wounded and thought himself to be dying, he *demonstrated servant leadership* by taking his place in line.

By forming and developing his Band of Brothers, Nelson had crafted the most effective fighting squadron the world's oceans had ever witnessed. When the moment of truth came, the hours of careful investment in developing other leaders paid off.

Summary

We close this instruction on Level 4 Leadership with a short summary, paraphrased from Paul David Tripp. Level 4 Leaders:

1. Love people
2. Know people
3. Speak truth into their lives
4. And help them lead where God has called them to lead.

CHAPTER 10

The Fifth Level of Influence: Developing Leaders Who Develop Leaders

Really great men have a curious feeling that the greatness is not in them, but through them.

—JOHN RUSKIN

The Fifth Level of Influence is the pinnacle of leadership ability. Whereas the influence of Level 3 Leaders lasts as long as the leader does and Level 4 Influence lasts as long as the leader's leaders are around, Level 5 Influence outlasts everybody. Level 5 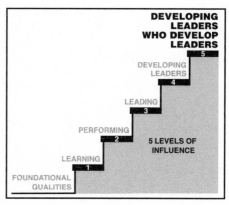 Influence is seen on those rare occasions when a leader not only becomes very accomplished as a leader himself and not only succeeds at developing other leaders, but manages to develop leaders who can then develop other leaders who continue the legacy onward. In history, Level 5 Influence has defined movements and ideas that echoed down through generations, profoundly impacting the world.

Our example of the soccer player gets stretched by the time Level 5 Influence is considered. Nevertheless, it is conceivable that the athlete not only matured into a great leader and coach, but became legendary as well. Perhaps she pioneered new techniques or training methods and revolutionized the entire sport. Her following among the world's soccer players became enormous, as those she developed in turn developed others. There would most likely be innovations named after her or perhaps even a professional team. At this point, her influence would have reached Level 5.

Presuppositions or the "Art" of Level 5

Level 5 Leaders understand:

1. Results will come through the endurance and succession of the vision.
2. The vision and the leader are intertwined.

Results Will Come Through the Endurance and Succession of the Vision

A Level 5 Leader can be identified by the magnitude of the following he or she leaves behind. The size of the vision, its enduring legacy, and successful continuation in the hands of other leaders is the fruit of a Level 5 Leader's efforts. Whereas Level 1 Leaders are only as good as what they learn, Level 2 Leaders are only as good as their personal performance, Level 3 Leaders are only as good as the performance of their team, Level 4 Leaders are only as good as the performance of their leaders, Level 5 Leaders are only as good as the enduring quality and succession of their vision.

The Vision and the Leader Are Intertwined

A Level 5 Leader is not only clear about the vision, and not even just capable of casting it before the organization, but he or she actually comes to embody that very vision. One cannot think of Martin Luther King, Jr. without thinking of the civil rights movement and his "I have a dream" vision for an America built on true equality of opportunity. The memory still rings sweet two generations later. His leadership attracted thousands of America's best and brightest leaders to a cause that burned in their hearts, produced changes in the laws of the United States, and taught leaders elsewhere how to protest peacefully, honorably, and successfully. His vision and example inspired later leaders and movements such as Nelson Mandela and the end of Apartheid in South Africa and Lech

> "If a man hasn't found something he is willing to die for, he isn't fit to live."

Walesa and the movement to free Poland from Soviet Communism. As King himself said, "If a man hasn't found something he is willing to die for, he isn't fit to live."

Level 5 Leaders get so wrapped up in their cause that they come to embody that very cause. The leader is almost lost inside the vision.

Actions or the "Science" of Level 5

At Level 5 Leadership there is not much science left; almost everything has become art. At Level 5, it's who the leader is and what he or she stands for, more than what the leader does, that makes the impact. This is one reason Level 5 Leaders are so rare.

Please don't misunderstand us here. Level 5 Leaders have been "doing" for a long time, probably their whole adult lives, in order

> *Level 5 Leaders surround themselves with leaders who have the potential of eclipsing their own personal glory.*

to reach this pinnacle of leadership impact. Their example has resonated and created a following of the highest caliber of leaders. Their very being has seemingly metastasized into the vision itself. Level 5 Leaders have decreased themselves, many times sacrificially, in order to increase the vision. As John the Baptist said when Jesus began his ministry, "I must decrease so that He can increase." Level 5 Leaders embody a similar sentiment. They must decrease in order for the cause to increase.

With all this said, there is one main action for Level 5 Leaders: attracting and developing the highest-caliber leaders available for the cause.

Attract the Highest-Caliber Leaders to the Cause

There comes a point in the development of other leaders where the mentor is limited by the attributes of the protégé. Becoming a Level 5 Leader requires followers who are at the Fourth Level of Influence, and many, many leaders will never even reach that height, but will instead plateau at the Third Level. So Level 5 Influence hinges on the ability of the leader to find people of the highest caliber to develop, and to retain them.

How are leaders of the highest caliber attracted in the first place? At this level of discussion, perks or incentives or great stock option plans will no longer do it. Top leadership talent is rarely attracted to such trinkets as a major point of focus. Instead, the top leaders in any field are attracted only by a strong and compelling vision, one they can believe in, one that provides room for them to make their mark, and one that speaks to their inner calling.

Finding Level 4 Leaders to develop requires a very mature, confident leader. At this Level of Influence, there is no room for ego or the petty jealousy of power that beset many leaders at the

Fourth or even the Third Levels of Influence. Level 5 Leadership requires that the leader surround himself with people of ability even higher than his own, which is opposite of human nature. Small leaders surround themselves with followers; big leaders surround themselves with other leaders. The biggest of all leaders, Level 5 Leaders, surround themselves with leaders who have the potential of eclipsing their own personal glory.

Napoleon Bonaparte, who was discussed briefly before, is a great example of a Level 3 Leader whose ego dictated that he surround himself with followers. His vision was one of personal glory, so he surrounded himself with sycophants: family members, yes-men, and followers who would not threaten his power. By doing this, Napoleon eliminated the sources of leadership ability that might have aided him in running his empire. He relied on people he had influence over rather than those he had respect for. This not only depleted his kingdom of leadership talent in most of its offices, but also produced a fear of initiative for those in authority. The commanding admirals who lost the two main sea battles in the war against England, the Battle of the Nile (depicted in the previous chapter) and later the Battle of Trafalgar, were paralyzed by their fear of Napoleon and afraid to take the initiative their leadership experience told them was prudent. This twice resulted in the destruction of the French navy and became the linchpin in Napoleon's ultimate defeat.

So to become a Level 5 Leader one must have his ego solidly in check, but that is not all. Leading Level 4 Leaders is not easy. By definition, Level 4 Leaders are strong and think for themselves. They have their own ideas and stand up firmly for what they believe. Richard Nixon observed, "If an individual wants to be a leader and isn't controversial, that means

"Consensus means that everybody agrees to say collectively what no one believes individually."

he never stood for anything." Consensus will rarely be present, which Level 5 Leaders know is a preferred condition. According to Abba Eban, "Consensus means that everybody agrees to say collectively what no one believes individually." So Level 5 Leaders must also be able to handle a bit of unrest as they let their Level 4 Leaders speak their minds and exercise decisions they think prudent.

This brings us to the topic of "meddling" or, as modern management theorists say, "micromanagement." Former president Jimmy Carter had one of the most unsuccessful administrations in presidential history. It had nothing to do with his character, as he is regarded by most as a decent and thoroughly honest man. However, his influence was severely limited by his inability to delegate authority and his obsessive need to be involved in every little detail of his administration. As President Dwight D. Eisenhower said, "A President who doesn't know how to decentralize will be weighed down with details and won't have time to deal with the big issues."

Perhaps the best contrast with Carter's style can be seen in his successor, Ronald Reagan. In *Ronald Reagan: How an Ordinary Man Became an Extraordinary Leader*, author Dinesh D'Souza describes a famous incident that occurred near the end of the Carter administration:

> Reagan had just been elected, and Carter felt it was important to brief him on some of the major issues that the new president would have to face. Carter went down the list, discussing various treaties and secret agreements the United States had with other countries. Reagan listened politely but did not write anything down or ask any questions. "The information was 'quite complex,'" Carter writes, "and I did not see how he could possibly retain all of it merely by listening."

Carter felt that the details mattered, and thus mastered them himself. Reagan left the details to his subordinates and focused on the big picture. The difference between the two presidents was more than just style; it was a difference in Leadership Level.

Level 5 Leaders must allow their Level 4 Leaders *to actually lead their leaders*, and to live and learn from their own results. A leader who meddles will never attract or retain the highest leadership talent because true leaders refuse to be "governed"; they will only agree, at the most, to be "guided."

Developing Leaders Who Develop Leaders: The Apostle Paul "An Influence of Inestimable Value"

He was a poor man, surviving on the generosity of his followers and his humble occupation of tent making. Conventional history has him small in stature, unimposing, and perhaps even slightly deformed. He was elected to no position, held no official authority, had no trappings of success. The man first known as Saul of Tarsus and later renamed Paul had none of the outward features the modern world thinks of when considering the term "leader," but he was, outside of Jesus, the greatest Level 5 Leader history has ever produced.

It was sometime around A.D. 64, and the setting was Rome, the very epicenter of the civilized world. Paul had been taken prisoner in Jerusalem and blamed with starting a riot in the temple there. He had been transported to Caesarea, a Roman city on the east coast of the Mediterranean Sea, to stand trial. He was tried by three separate Roman officials, who each to some extent were personally affected by his testimony, and was retained there for over two years. At some point in the proceedings, Paul evoked his rights to freedom of religion as a Roman citizen, which necessitated his appearance in the capital city of Rome to stand further trial. A treacherous sea voyage resulted in a shipwreck on the shores of the island of Malta. That following spring, after the winter storms had subsided, Paul was finally taken to Rome to stand trial, quite possibly in front of the ruthless Emperor Nero himself.

He would have to wait, though, and was placed under house arrest for another two years.

This grand imprisonment and adventure followed a life of hardships and persecution. In Paul's own words, "Five times I received forty stripes [whippings] save one. Thrice was I beaten with rods, once was I stoned, thrice I suffered shipwreck, a night and a day I have been in the deep; In journeying often, in perils of waters, in perils of robbers, in perils by mine own countrymen, in perils by the heathen, in perils in the city, in perils in the wilderness, in perils in the sea, in perils among false brethren; in weariness and painfulness, in watching often, in hunger and thirst, in fastings often, in cold and nakedness" (2 Corinthians 11:24–28).

He had traveled extensively, ignoring these perils to his person, pursuing one great, bold vision of spreading the news of Christ's death and resurrection to the world. All along the way he had taken companions. These men he taught and trained in the arts of leadership, teaching them about his great faith in Christ and the importance of their sacrifice as servant leaders to spread the word of the gospel throughout the then civilized world. He had "planted" churches in cities from Asia Minor to Macedonia, in the important city of Ephesus and the debauched city of Corinth, and in one of the ancient world's most advanced metropolises, the city of Antioch. Perhaps most remarkably, as a result of his long imprisonment there, an active, thriving church was begun right in Rome, the seat of the government of the empire and center of pagan religions.

Further, he created the opportunity to teach and debate the finest minds in the world, in Athens, the centerpiece of intellectual thought and home of philosophy. At each location he had schooled entire groups of leaders and followers to carry on the great work after he had moved on. He wrote profusely—instructing, teaching, rebuking, counseling, and coaching through letters that were delivered by his private couriers. According to Albert

Barnes, author of *The Life of the Apostle Paul*, "No less than thirteen, and probably fourteen out of the twenty-seven books of the New Testament were written by him, or at his dictation." These writings served not only as continuing guidance to his leaders, who, at the time, were spread out around the Roman Empire, but became guideposts to millions of followers the world over, down through the next two millennia.

With all that he had done, however, many look upon Paul's trial before the rulers of Rome as his high-water mark. According to author John MacArthur in *The Book on Leadership*, "That moment was, in effect, the pinnacle of Paul's ministry and the fulfillment of his deepest desire. He was called to be the apostle to the Gentiles. Rome was the cosmopolitan center of the pagan world. Paul had long sought an opportunity to preach the gospel in such a venue before the world's most important political leaders and philosophical trendsetters. This was that opportunity." Paul's vision had taken him into the very eye of the storm, where he courageously faced up to the duty of his calling.

By Paul's own account, after this "first trial" he was "delivered from the mouth of the lion" and set free. There are many conjectures about his further travels into Spain and again into Macedonia. Soon enough, most likely as part of the massive Christian persecution following the burning of Rome (started by Nero himself to clear the way for the building of a great temple and conveniently blamed on the Christians), Paul was again imprisoned in Rome. This time, however, there would be no amiable conditions of "house arrest." He was placed in a damp, dark hole in the ground, according to historical legend, in the base of the Mamertine Prison. Here he wrote his final letters while awaiting execution. At that point, Paul's whereabouts and activities vanish from the record. Most likely he was beheaded just outside Rome on the Ostian Way.

The man had perished, but his work lived on. In the years

following Paul's death, the churches he and his followers had started flourished and grew, reaching out around the countryside and starting other churches.

Paul had left behind a host of other leaders to carry on his vision. His main protégé, Timothy, was the recipient of two specific letters. Paul wrote these letters "in order to pass the mantle of church leadership to his young protégé," said John MacArthur. "He regarded Timothy as a clone of himself, a carbon copy of his leadership." There was also Titus, a man who could equip and train other leaders. When Paul wrote the epistle to Titus, this leader was at that time leading the church on the island of Crete, which Paul had planted. In that epistle (Titus 1:5) Paul writes, "For this reason I left you in Crete, that you should set in order the things that are lacking, and appoint elders in every city as I commanded you."

The appointment of elders in every city was a specific, deliberate process of finding, developing, and empowering leaders across the lands to carry on the vision of spreading the gospel of Christ. Then there was Luke, Paul's personal attendant. Luke was shipwrecked with Paul and was imprisoned with him. Paul charged Luke with writing histories and accounts of the gospel message, which resulted in two books of the New Testament, Luke and Acts. Mark was a young protégé who had gotten off to a rocky start. Once severely disappointing Paul, Mark later became "useful for ministry" and was recommended by Paul for leadership. In his letters, Paul mentions other names of those involved in the spread of the early church, and there are perhaps thousands who have gone unnamed.

Both the named and the unnamed became a dynamic legacy to the Level 5 Leadership of the Apostle Paul. He deliberately and painstakingly established followers of leaders across the landscape of the ancient world, establishing a church structure that would train and develop more and more leaders to carry the gospel to the ends of the earth. And that they did. Among the early churches were those in the cities of Troas, Assos, Mitylene, Pergamum, Thyatira, Sardis, Philadelphia, Hierapolis, Smyrna, Magnesia, Miletus, Ephesus, Cos, Cnidus, Rhodes, Myra, Attalia, Perga, Lystra, Iconium, Colossae, Laodicea, Derbe, Seleucia (both in Asia Minor and in present-day Syria), Tarsus (Paul's hometown), Salamis, and Paphos. By the end of the first century, only roughly forty years after Paul's death, this list of churches throughout Asia Minor and Greece and in Rome, Puteoli, and around the Bay of Naples had grown even more.

By the end of the third century, Paul's leaders and their descendants, as well as those of the original apostles, had spread the gospel message of Christ as far north as Britannia (modern-day England) and as far west as the Iberian Peninsula (modern-day Spain and Portugal), and even into northern Africa. Perhaps the most indicative sign of the permeation of Christianity throughout the world is the decision of Roman emperor Constantine in A.D. 312 to embrace Christianity. By the end of the fourth century, Christianity would become the official religion of the Roman Empire, the same empire that had executed Paul!

Today, Christianity is the dominant religion in the North American, South American, European, and Australian continents, and is growing most rapidly throughout Russia, China, and many parts of Africa. This is all occurring in places where Paul never traveled and in the lives of people Paul never met, centuries after he lived! That is indicative of the influence of Level 5 Leadership. (*Visions outlive them, grow into movements, and carry on through others over time.*) According to Albert Barnes, "There has been no one of our race who has done so much to determine the theological opinions of mankind as Paul has done." Paul's vision of Christianity spreading throughout the world became so strong, so real, and so enduring that it is impossible to consider Paul without also thinking of his cause. (*The leader grows into his mission.*)

As can be said of the causes and visions of true Level 5 Leaders, the world will never be the same.

Summary

Level 5 Leadership is about making a difference in the status quo that outlives the leader. Level 5 Leaders begin by attracting, inspiring, and enabling leaders who are adept at developing *other* leaders. Only the strongest, humblest, most secure, visionary leaders ever reach this pinnacle of leadership. The results of such ability are astronomical. In *The Effective Executive*, Peter Drucker said, "[No] executive has ever suffered because his subordinates were strong and effective. There is no prouder boast, but also no better prescription, for executive effectiveness than the words Andrew Carnegie, the father of the U.S. steel industry, chose for his own tombstone: 'Here lies a man who knew how to bring into his service men better than he was himself.'"

This chapter and the summary of the life of the Apostle Paul demonstrate that Level 5 Leaders are rare among us. A Level 5 Leader is in a league of his own. He commands the forces of powerful Level 4 Leaders in a productive direction, he's "on fire" for an enormous vision that embraces all of his collective energies, and he leaves a true legacy on the earth. Level 5 is a measure of influence to which every truly inspired, cause-driven, vision-pursuing leader should aspire.

Conclusion

Understanding the Five Levels of Influence

The concept of the Five Levels of Influence is especially helpful for many reasons. First, it helps an individual gauge his own ability and understand how and where to improve. Second, it helps a leader understand where people are in terms of ability and what to do to help them develop. Third, it assists a leader in evaluating the Leadership Level that exists in any portion of his or her *organization*.

Understanding this information about self, people, and organizations becomes extremely helpful in diagnosing issues and providing guidance, correction, and direction. For example, if an individual feels she is at Level 2, she knows what to work on to attain Level 3. If a particular person is performing at Level 2, then the leader must preside at Level 3. If a division is performing at Level 3, the leader must provide Level 4 Leadership, and so on.

The various Levels of Influence also serve to illustrate the concept of the "ability to influence" through the correct actions of a leader. At Level 1 there is no influence, except upon the budding leader himself. At Level 2 the influence can be considered to be "addition," as the efforts of the individual are all that's added to the organization. Level 3 can be thought of as "multiplication" because now the contribution is amplified through a team. Level 4 would then be "exponential" impact because leaders are affecting other leaders, who then lead teams. Level 5 is beyond mathematical description and can only be called a "revolution."

The Results of Leadership

Colin Powell, hero of Desert Storm and former secretary of state, observed that "there are no secrets to success. It is the result of preparation, hard work, and learning from failure." The same could be said of leadership. There are no secrets. It will take work. It will take preparation. There will be failures. The lessons from those failures must be understood. In essence, the leader must grow.

There is a conversation in the novel *The Sun Also Rises*, by Ernest Hemingway, in which one character says to another, "How did you go bankrupt?" to which the response is, "Gradually, then suddenly." The compounding effect of leadership is much the same. At first influence seems very gradual, and even non-existent, as the leader or the organization enters the learning phase. Then, ever so subtly, performance improves. Out of that performance, leaders arise. From that leadership emerges a few who can lead other leaders. And then, *suddenly*, the results are astronomical.

The point is that leadership is a process. It is ongoing and compounding. It doesn't happen overnight, but over time, it happens in undeniable ways.

Walk a Mile, See a Mile Farther

Everybody comes onto the leadership playing field with a different set of innate abilities, but everyone can improve those abilities. The vital component of leadership effectiveness is continual personal growth.

The concept of leadership, which appears so daunting and intimidating to so many people, will become clearer and clearer as the stairs of the Five Levels of Influence are ascended. As the physicist Edward Teller said, "No endeavor that is worthwhile is simple in prospect; [but] if it is right, it will be simple in retrospect." The leadership journey is not clear when one embarks upon it; but with seasoning, experience, growth in influence, and knowledge, the way becomes clearer. With each new mile traveled, the next mile comes into view. Studying the Five Levels of Influence clears the fog, maps the journey, and allows the aspiring leader to see farther into his own future.

Calling All Leaders

Becoming a leader should not frighten anyone—it should inspire. Leadership is one of the most rewarding endeavors known to mankind. It is also one of the most important.

> *"The only way for evil to flourish is for good men to do nothing."*

Our society is suffering from a leadership crisis. As Edmund Burke noted a century ago, "The only way for evil to flourish is for good men to do nothing." There are too many people sitting idly, while the world cries out for leadership. We need leaders in the government, leaders in business, leaders in the community, leaders in the schools, leaders in the homes, and leaders in the churches.

Author Gil Bailie wrote, "Don't ask yourself what the world needs. Ask yourself what makes you come alive, and go do that, because what the world needs is people who have come alive."

Leaders are born every place where somebody comes alive.

That's the key to discovering your own leadership calling: find out what makes you come alive.

Albert Schweitzer believed, "The tragedy of life is what dies inside a man while he lives." Leaders don't allow that tragedy. They live while they are alive.

Ultimately, leadership is a personal responsibility. You have to figure it out as you go, but don't worry: God won't give you a vision without a means to accomplish it.

So come alive.

Get to work.

Lead!

BIBLIOGRAPHY

Abrashoff, Captain D. Michael. *It's Your Ship: Management Techniques from the Best Damn Ship in the Navy*. New York: Warner Business Books, 2002.

Ambrose, Stephen. *Band of Brothers: E Company, 506th Regiment, 101st Airborne from Normandy to Hitler's Eagle's Nest*. New York: Simon & Schuster, 1992.

Attner, Paul. "Right of Way." *Sporting News*, St. Louis: Vulcan Sports Media, Inc., December 13, 2004, p.26.

Autry, James A. *The Servant Leader: How to Build a Creative Team, Develop Great Morale, and Improve Bottom-Line Performance*. New York: Three Rivers Press, 2004.

Axelrod, Alan. *Profiles in Leadership*. New York: Prentice Hall Press, 2003.

Barna, George. *A Fish Out of Water: 9 Strategies to Maximize Your God-Given Leadership Potential*. Nashville: Integrity Publishers, 2002.

————. *Leaders on Leadership: Wisdom, Advice and Encouragement on the Art of Leading God's People*. Ventura: Regal Books, 1997.

Barnes, Albert. *The Life of the Apostle Paul*. Grand Rapids: Baker Books, 1996.

Beliles, Mark A., and Stephen K. McDowell. *America's Providential History*. Charlottesville: Providence Foundation, 1989.

Boettner, Loraine. *The Reformed Doctrine of Predestination*. The Presbyterian and Reformed Publishing Company, 1974.

Brands, H. W. *Andrew Jackson*. New York: Doubleday, 2005.

————. *The First American: The Life and Times of Benjamin Franklin*. New York: Doubleday, 2000.

Bruce, F. F. *In the Steps of the Apostle Paul*. Grand Rapids: Kregel Publications, 1995.

Bush, George W. *A Charge to Keep: My Journey to the White House*. New York: HarperCollins Publishers, 1999.

Callo, Joseph F. *Legacy of Leadership: Lessons from Admiral Lord Nelson*. Oregon: Hellgate Press, 1999.

Carnegie, Dale. *How to Win Friends and Influence People*. New York: Simon & Schuster, 1936.

Carter, Andre. "Lord of the Rings: Tom Brady Has Two Super Bowl Rings. He Wants More." *Sports Illustrated for Kids*, New York: Time, Inc.: September 2004, p. 26.

Collins, Jim. *Good to Great: Why Some Companies Make the Leap . . . and Others Don't*. New York: HarperCollins Publishers, 2001.

Covey, Stephen R. *The 7 Habits of Highly Effective People: Powerful Lessons in Personal Change*. New York: Simon & Schuster, 1989.

Csorba, Les T. *Trust: The One Thing That Makes or Breaks a Leader*. Nashville: Nelson Publishers, 2004.

D'Souza, Dinesh. *Ronald Reagan: How an Ordinary Man Became an Extraordinary Leader*. New York: Simon & Schuster, 1997.

Dorman, Henry O. *The Speaker's Book of Quotations*. New York: Ballantine Books, 1987.

Dowley, Tim. *The Baker Atlas of Christian History*. Grand Rapids: Baker Books, 1996.

Eldredge, John. *Wild at Heart: Discovering the Secret of a Man's Soul*. Nashville: Thomas Nelson Publishers, 2001.

Eng, Steve. *Jimmy Buffett: The Man from Margaritaville Revealed*. New York: St. Martin's Press, 1996.

Flexner, James Thomas. *Washington: The Indispensable Man*. New York: Little, Brown and Company, 1969.

Franklin, Benjamin. *Autobiography and Other Writings*. Oxford: Oxford University Press, 1993.

George, Bill. *Authentic Leadership: Rediscovering the Secrets to Creating Lasting Value*. San Francisco: Jossey-Bass, 2003.

Gerber, Michael E. *The E Myth Revisited*. New York: HarperCollins Publishers, 1995.

Gilbert, Martin. *Churchill: A Life*. New York: Henry Holt and Company, 1991.

Godin, Seth. *The Purple Cow: Transform Your Business by Being Remarkable*. New York: Penguin Group, 2002.

Guinness, Os. *Character Counts*. Grand Rapids: Baker Books, 1999.

Hanson, Neil. *The Confident Hope of a Miracle*. New York: Vintage Books, 2003.

Hayward, Steven F. *Churchill on Leadership: Executive Success in the Face of Adversity*. Rocklin: Prima Publishing, 1997.

Herman, Arthur. *To Rule the Waves: How the British Navy Shaped the Modern World*. New York: HarperCollins Publishers, 2004.

Holtz, Lou, and Harvey Mackay. *Winning Every Day: The Game Plan for Success*. New York: HarperCollins Publishers, 1998.

Hunter, James C. *The Servant: A Simple Story about the True Essence of Leadership*. Roseville: Prima Publishing, 1998.

———. *The World's Most Powerful Leadership Principle: How to Become a Servant Leader*. New York: Crown Business, 2004.

Kaltman, Al. *Cigars, Whiskey & Winning: Leadership Lessons from General Ulysses S. Grant*. New Jersey: Prentice Hall Press, 1998.

Keller, Jeff. *Attitude Is Everything: Change Your Attitude . . . And You Change Your Life!* Tampa: INTI Publishing, 1999.

Kouzes, James, and Barry Posner. *The Leadership Challenge*. San Francisco: Jossey-Bass, 2002.

Krzyzewski, Mike, with Donald T. Phillips. *Leading with the Heart: Coach K's Successful Strategies for Basketball, Business, and Life*. New York: Warner Books, 2000.

Love, John. *McDonald's: Behind the Arches*. New York: Bantam Books, 1986.

MacArthur, John. *The Book on Leadership*. Nashville: Nelson Books, 2004.

Maxwell, John C. *Equipping 101: What Every Leader Needs to Know.* Nashville: Thomas Nelson Publishers, 2003.

———. *The 21 Irrefutable Laws of Leadership: Follow Them and People Will Follow You.* Nashville, Thomas Nelson Publishers, 1998.

McLellan, Vern. *Wise Words and Quotes.* Wheaton: Tyndale House Publishers, Inc., 1998.

McCormack, John, and David R. Legge. *Self-Made in America: Plain Talk for Plain People about the Meaning of Success.* New York: Addison-Wesley Publishing Company, 1990.

McDowell, Josh, and Bob Hostetler. *The New Tolerance.* Wheaton: Tyndale, 1998.

Mesiti, Pat. *Attitudes and Altitudes: The Principles, Practice and Profile of 21st-Century Leadership.* Anaheim: KNI Incorporated, 1997.

Miller, Nathan. *Broadsides: The Age of Fighting Sail, 1775-1815.* New York: John Wiley & Sons, Inc., 2000.

Morris, Edmund. *The Rise of Theodore Roosevelt.* New York: Ballantine Books, 1979.

O'Leary, Jeff. *The Centurion Principles: Battlefield Lessons for Frontline Leaders.* Nashville: Thomas Nelson, Inc., 2004.

O'Neil, William J. *Military and Political Leaders & Success: 55 Top Military and Political Leaders & How They Achieved Greatness.* New York: McGraw-Hill, 2005.

Perot, Ross. *My Life & The Principles for Success.* Arlington: The Summit Publishing Group, 1996.

Phillips, Donald, T. *Lincoln on Leadership: Executive Strategies for Tough Times*. New York: Warner Books, 1992.

———. *The Founding Fathers on Leadership: Classic Teamwork in Changing Times*. New York: Warner Books, 1997.

Randall, Willard Sterne. *George Washington: A Life*. New York: Henry Holt and Company, 1997.

Remini, Robert V. *The Life of Andrew Jackson*. New York: Harper & Row Publishers, 1988.

Robbins, Anthony. *Awaken the Giant Within: How to Take Immediate Control of Your Mental, Emotional, Physical & Financial Destiny!* New York: Simon & Schuster, 1991.

Roberts, Wess. *The Best Advice Ever for Leaders*. Kansas City: Andrews McMeel Publishing, 2002.

Roosevelt, Theodore. *An Autobiography*. New York: Da Capo Press, 1913.

Schefter, Adam. "Brady Is a Man in Charge of His Future." NFL Network, Jacksonville: NFL.com, February 6, 2005.

Schom, Alan. *Napoleon Bonaparte*. New York: HarperCollins Publishers, 1997.

Schwartz, David J. *The Magic of Thinking Big*. New York: Prentice Hall, 1959.

Shanahan, Mike, and Adam Schefter. *Think Like a Champion: Building Success One Victory at a Time*. New York: HarperCollins Publishers, 1999.

Shirer, William L. *The Rise and Fall of the Third Reich*. New York: Simon & Schuster, 1960.

Slater, Robert. *The Wal-Mart Decade: How a Generation of Leaders*

Turned Sam Walton's Legacy into the World's #1 Company. New York: Penguin Group, 2003.

Stanley, Andy. *The Next Generation Leader: 5 Essentials for Those Who Will Shape the Future.* Oregon: Multnomah Publishers, Inc., 2003.

Strock, James M. *Theodore Roosevelt on Leadership.* Roseville: Prima Publishing, 2001.

Summitt, Pat, with Sally Jenkins. *Reach for the Summit: The Definite Dozen System for Succeeding at Whatever You Do.* New York: Broadway Books, 1998.

Tedlow, Richard S. *Giants of Enterprise: Seven Business Innovators and the Empires They Built.* New York: HarperCollins Publishers, 2003.

Thorpe, Scott. *Revolutionary Strategies of the Founding Fathers: Leadership Lessons from America's Most Successful Patriots.* Naperville: SourceBooks, Inc., 2003.

Tichy, Noel M. *The Leadership Engine: How Winning Companies Build Leaders at Every Level.* New York: HarperCollins, 1997.

Tichy, Noel M., and Nancy Cardwell. *The Cycle of Leadership: How Great Leaders Teach Their Companies to Win.* New York: HarperCollins, 2002.

Walton, Sam, and John Huey. *Sam Walton: Made in America. My Story.* New York: Doubleday, 1992.

Welch, Jack, and John A. Byrne. *Jack: Straight from the Gut.* New York: Warner Business Books, 2001.

Weller, Bob. *The Dreamweaver: The Story of Mel Fisher and his Quest for the Treasure of the Spanish Galleon* Atocha. Charleston: Fletcher and Fletcher Publishing, 1996.

White, Colin. *Nelson: A Pitkin Biographical Guide*. Great Britain, 2003.

Williams, Pat. *The Paradox of Power: A Transforming View of Leadership*. New York: Warner Faith, 2002.

Willis, Stevenson. *The Proverbs of Leadership: Principles for Leading Your People to the Pinnacle of Greatness*. Nashville: Pillar Press, 2002.

Wooden, John, and Steve Jamison. *Wooden: A Lifetime of Observations and Reflections On and Off the Court*. Chicago: Contemporary Books, 1997.

INDEX

CHRIS BRADY

Mr. Brady was educated in engineering with a bachelor of science degree in mechanical engineering from Kettering University (formerly GMI) and a master's in manufacturing systems engineering on fellowship from Carnegie-Mellon University. He conducted his master's thesis at Toyohashi University in Japan. Mr. Brady is an avid pilot and boater, and enjoys nearly every form of motorized adventure.